"THE MOST BRILLIANT INCIDENT IN THE HISTORY OF THE ANTARCTIC
. . . Sir Ernest Shackleton's journey is one of the most wonderful achievements in Polar exploration. His name will always be written in the annals of the Antarctic in letters of fire."

> **—Roald Amundsen**
> **Discoverer of the South Pole**

"A giant of a man, a gallant man, endowed with audacity and exuberance . . . Shackleton's journey was distinguished by a display of courage and endurance and, on Shackleton's part, of power of leadership unparalleled in Polar exploration."

> **—L. P. Kirwan**
> **Director, Royal Geographic Society**

"Shackleton had genius . . . the men loved him and would follow him anywhere."

> **—Frank Arthur Worsley**
> **Member of the crew on Shackleton's incredible voyage**

SHACKLETON'S VOYAGE

Donald Barr Chidsey

AWARD BOOKS
NEW YORK

SHACKLETON'S VOYAGE

CHAPTER 1

IT WAS the last day of 1902, and three men standing in an icy waste shook their heads, they knew they could not go on.

They had reckoned their latitude at 82 degrees 16 minutes, farther south than any human being had ever gone before—within a little over 300 miles from the South Pole. To go any farther would be suicide. So they shook their heads, and made camp.

The leader, Robert Falcon Scott, was a commander in the British Royal Navy, a thoughtful, shy, reserved man—Old Moony they had called him at the naval academy—with no sense of humor but a very high sense of duty. He was emotional: "He cried more easily than any man I have ever known," his friend Apsley Cherry-Garrard said of him.

E. A. "Billy" Wilson was a physician, naturalist, and artist—he repeatedly risked frostbite when he took off his gloves to sketch the mountains they were passing—and a man of considerable culture. He and Commander Scott were close personal friends.

7

The third member of the group, Ernest Henry Shackleton, wrote in his diary that night: "Last day of the old year and today we turned back after a blowy night. The dogs are awful, not pulling at all. Clarence gave up the ghost today. Camped two P.M. Went on skis to try and land full of crevasses. No go. Wonderful sight."

Shackleton had been a school dropout at 16, but he was far from being a stupid man. At 28, he was the youngest member of the party—Scott was 34, Wilson 30. The son of a physician, Shackleton held a master's certificate in the merchant marine and was a competent navigator. He was a clear and forceful speaker. He wrote well too, though it must be admitted that his punctuation left much to be desired.

There was nothing to guide these men. There were no precedents, no records. Nobody had ever been anywhere near the place where they camped. Previous explorers had but nibbled at the edges of this continent, the very existence of which had only recently been confirmed. Nobody had plunged into the terrible interior as these men had done.

The dogs, it was agreed, were the greatest disappointment. All three men had been accustomed, at home, to having friendly relations with their own and their neighbors' dogs, which were like members of the family. They had learned, however, that Eskimo dogs were something different. Eskimo dogs were snappish, they fought among themselves. They were soon divided into two classes—the pullers, which headed the various teams, and the others, which were called "sooners" because, it was explained, they would sooner do anything else than pull. They needed to be handled with severity. Though they were all given names—"Clarence" in Shackleton's diary entry was a dog—that was as far as intimacy went.

When this little expedition had left the supply ship and base camp on the shores of McMurdo Sound on November 2nd, it had taken five sledges loaded with supplies and pulled by all the dogs present, 19 in number. It now had three sledges, one of which it was prepared to abandon within a few days, and half a dozen dogs, all sooners. Some dogs had died of a strange ailment that probably was a form of scurvy. Others, having demonstrated that they could no longer do their share of the work, had been shot, and their bodies had been served to the rest, which were thus temporarily revived by fresh meat. Shackleton and Dr. Wilson had to do this dirty work. Not that Commander Scott was a man to shirk any job; he just couldn't stand the sight of blood.

It was not altogether the dogs' fault. They had started well, even spiritedly, chasing the two supporting parties. But when those supporting parties had turned back, and the dogs had nothing before them but blank snow and ice, they became discouraged.

They also became ill. Their regular diet consisted of dried fish that had been brought all the way from England for this specific purpose. In

9

the process it had necessarily passed through the tropics, and may have become contaminated.

There was another possibility. The weather in Antarctica is always unpredictable, but at least the temperature in the interior seldom gets as high as zero Fahrenheit, even in midsummer, which is January. Yet soon after this expedition started forth it had encountered what for that part of the world virtually amounted to a tropical heat wave. The temperature on one memorable day had soared to 20 degrees *above* zero. To be sure, it had quickly returned to the more customary 30 to 40 degrees below, where it was now; but perhaps in that unaccountable warm spell, some definite damage had been done to the dried fish.

Whatever the reason, the dogs were not pulling their weight.

Ernest Henry Shackleton, the morning that they broke their farthest-out camp and turned north again, had something more than the dogs to worry him. His scurvy was returning, worse than ever. Perhaps *he* couldn't pull his weight, either.

CHAPTER 2

HE TRIED to act as if nothing was the matter, but in the backbreaking work of hauling the sledges and in the close quarters of their tent at night—barely room for the three of them to stretch out in their separate sleeping bags—he knew that the symptoms would catch the eye of Dr. Wilson, especially when his gums began to bleed.

Those symptoms—listlessness, weakness, short-windedness—had been noted previously on the way south, and even Commander Scott had displayed them slightly. Only the physician seemed to be immune. The symptoms had passed away, hopefully for good, but now they had returned, redoubled in intensity.

The pain was mental as well. Shackleton had tried hard to get on this expedition, a semi-official one made up largely of regular Navy men. He had been turned down on his first application, as a mere merchant marine man, not even a reservist, and it was only after he had exerted influence through the father of a friend, a large contributor to the expedition, that he was accepted as third officer. He was keenly conscious of this, and believed that the others were too. Always a hard worker, he had worked harder than ever on the long voyage and in the field. And now, at the most telling time of all, the return from their historic dash, he was about to let his companions down.

In addition, the malady was embarrassing. A scurvy victim's breath stinks worse and worse as the disease intensifies; and it was a very small tent they had.

In the old days scurvy had been the curse of seamen. After months without fresh food, mariners were particularly susceptible to it, though the disease would sometimes break out in jails as well. It was popularly supposed that scurvy had been eradicated after Captain James Cook in the 1770's took his men around the world without a single case of it. He had been careful to keep them in fresh food, serving out daily rations of lime juice when there was nothing else, a trick the Royal Navy and soon afterward the British merchant marine were quick to pick up, with the result that British tars came to be known as lime juicers or limeys. Scurvy, however, had simply gone underground. Given a chance to emerge, it could still be deadly. It was the dread of polar explorers. Along the shores of Antarctica a man could kill a seal now and then, or some penguins. In the interior there was nothing—no kind of animal or vegetable life at all.

Some of the time Shackleton, who was passionately fond of poetry and could pen pretty good verse himself, recited, in his mind, his favorite fragments of Browning and Keats. There was no daytime conversation, only shouted orders, for the wind, the snow, and the hard pulling discouraged this. And at night in the tent Shackleton, ordinarily a chatty, sociable sort, tried to keep his mouth shut, he was so conscious of his breath.

"Tennyson's 'Ulysses' keeps running through my head," he confided to his diary the night of January 6th.

Most of the time, though, like the others, he thought only of food, planning tremendous, rich meals that never would be served. They were obsessed by memories of food.

The dash had been carefully planned. When they pulled out of base camp they had 1,850 pounds of food and equipment, packed on five sledges. The food part of this, besides the dog food, was enough to allow each man one and a half pounds a day for nine weeks, though Scott hoped that because of the two supporting parties and the depots that they set up along the route he might be able to stretch this to 13 weeks.

Two things they had not counted on.

The southing in many places had been so steep that dogs and men together could not haul the heavily laden sledges, and repeatedly this had to be done by relays—that is, by dumping half a load, hauling the rest a mile or so and dumping it, then going back for the first half-load. This took time, and it was trying on men and dogs alike.

The other thing they had not anticipated was

the quick ending of the dogs' endurance. They shot the last two worthless ones January 14th, but did not eat them. They jettisoned the dogs' food rations, thus lightening the load a little.

The wind was often from the south now—that is, at their backs—and they saved a little labor from time to time by rigging their tent as a sail. Mostly, however, it was a case of chest harness and a low-leaning pull.

Their own food supplies were scanty, and they cut their daily allowance once again. Each got the same, every day. Scott and Wilson were smallish men, but Shackleton, though he stood only five feet ten, looked taller, and though he had small hands and feet and narrow wrists and ankles, he was broad across the shoulders, deep in the chest, a very strong man. There was more of him to feed, and it may be that this is why he succumbed earlier to scurvy. By this time Scott and Wilson were showing signs of the same ailment, but they were not as desperately ill as Shackleton was.

His condition of course had been noted, and Wilson told Scott that he didn't think Shackleton would survive the dash. He didn't know this man, a tough nut if ever there was one.

Scott took Shackleton aside and told him that in no circumstances was he to do any further hauling, and that if he felt like it he could ride. Shackleton declined this. Scott also told him that he was to rest whenever they stopped; he was not to do any camp duties. It was humiliating.

Wilson sketched no more. They gathered no

additional rock samples. Their whole aim in life now was to raise the flag-marked Depot B and after that Depot A and then the camp. To miss either depot would mean sure death.

They made it, somehow. They stumbled into Depot B, then into Depot A, and on February 3rd, 1903, the base on McMurdo Sound, where they saw that a relief ship, *Morning*, had arrived on schedule. They had travelled 950 miles, though because of the relaying they had not penetrated half that many miles into Antarctica. They had been gone for 93 days.

Then came the most unkindest cut of all. The expedition, as such, was due to remain in this base camp all winter, and it would undoubtedly make other forays into the interior the following summer; but after a few days of rest and food, Commander Scott announced to Ernest Henry Shackleton that he was sending him back to England on the *Morning*. He had been tried (though Scott didn't put it this way) and found wanting.

Shackleton seethed, but contained his fury. He vowed to himself when he went aboard the relief ship that he would outlive both Wilson and Scott. He did.

CHAPTER 3

SHACKLETON had found his metier. He had come to life. He had always been a physically vibrant person—boxing, football, rugby, swimming—but until he was returned from Antarctica his dreams and desires, though grand enough, had been amorphous. Now at last he knew what he wanted.

Though his name was English, Shackleton had spent his early boyhood in Ireland, where the family had been living for several generations. When the family moved to England, to Sydenham, the boys at the day school, Dulwich, called him Mick because of a trace of brogue in his speech. He had a brother, much younger, and many sisters. He got along all right with almost everybody.

He was incurably—and exuberantly—romantic. He loved sea stories, ate up Jules Verne, and learned whole pages of Sir Walter Scott not by memory but by heart, which is something else again. While still in his teens he could complete almost any quotation you started, provided it was of the English romantic school of poetry. Tennyson was his favorite—at first.

He did not run away to sea, as incorrigible mythmakers were fond of saying. Dr. Shackleton was doing well, but the house in Sydenham, what with all those daughters, was mighty crowded, and young Ernest had not covered himself with honors at Dulwich and was hardly to be considered university material. There was a family conference, at which Ernest mentioned the sea, and his father arranged to get him a post as boy with the privileges and prerogatives of an apprentice, on probation, aboard a North-Western Shipping Company vessel. He was 16.

He was seasick the first three days, and voluble and inquisitive after that, a hard worker, a good companion. His practice of reading the Bible every night did disconcert his fellow apprentices, but they got used to it. He liked to sing, though he didn't have much of a voice. He might have been a mite odd, but there was nothing creepy about him.

He served his apprenticeship in sail, not because he had any thought that a working knowledge of canvas might come in handy if ever he embarked upon a polar voyage—nothing was further from his mind—but purely and simply because it was the custom of the time in the merchant marine; and as soon as he won his second mate's license in London, October 4, 1894, after some private tutoring, he switched to steam.

Holding a second mate's license did not mean getting a second mate's berth, and for some years young Shackleton was third mate or even fourth mate on a series of slow, undistinguished hookers, carrying unexciting cargos like rice, hemp, guano, to remote parts of the world—Yokohama, Saigon, Capetown, Sydney, Valparaiso. At no time during this period did he cross either the Arctic or the Antarctic circles, though once when he was still an apprentice he did round the Horn.

A naval court in Singapore, April 28th, 1898, awarded him his master's certificate, but it might be years before he got a command—if he ever got one at all.

It was at this stage of his career that he fell head-over-heels in love.

Emily Dorman was tall, lovely to look at, and several years older than Ernest Henry Shackleton. Like him, she came from a large and happy family, and he met her because she was a friend of one of his sisters. She was the daughter of a successful solicitor and rich in her own right.

There was nothing indirect about this man, nothing oblique or circuitous, and he saw right away that he wanted Emily for his wife. But he also saw that he was not in a position to keep her in the style to which she was accustomed. He must do bigger things, in order to be worthy of her. He must do *very* big things. He must *be* somebody. He had high-flown ideas.

The lady was not so confident. It was scarcely a whirlwind courtship, for she shillied and shallied as she regarded this impetuous young man from a freighter and wondered if maybe she had been unwise when she turned down sundry earlier and more prosperous wooers.

Though she was for some time undecided, they were both serious about it. Shackleton, who in some ways was touchingly old-fashioned, wrote a fine, manly, if somewhat ungrammatical letter to her father, expressing the wish and the belief that Emily would sooner or later accept him, confessing that he did not have the means to support her as she deserved to be supported, but praying anyway for the father's blessing, provided always, of course, that Emily eventually did say yes. The father granted this.

Shackleton would not touch her money. He was much too proud for that.

Since he was so often away, in the Orient, in India, or in South America, they did not have much time together. They made the most of what they did have. They visited the National Gallery, they visited the British Museum, and they talked and talked and talked about poetry.

Her favorite was Browning; but Shackleton, who was in a Swinburne period just then, feared that he never had thought much of Browning. Shocked, she converted him. It was a real revelation, not a pretense in order that he might get into the good graces of this girl. For the rest of his life he quoted Browning by the hour. He came to love him as much as Tennyson—in some ways, perhaps, even more.

But this wasn't being appointed to directorships. This wasn't making a name for himself. Browning was sweet to the ear—even sweeter, he was prepared to concede, than Swinburne—but Browning was not a house in the country.

He burned with impatience. He must prove himself.

There was no secret about the Antarctic expedition that was being organized. The papers were full of it. The Royal Society and the Royal Geographic Society were doing everything in their power to promote it. Rich men were contributing, with or without strings. The government had promised to pick up a large part of the tab. The *Discovery* was being built. The Navy would cooperate. Robert Falcon Scott, amid salvos of applause, was named as leader. The wonder was that this project had not earlier caught the desperate eye of a romantic young man in search of adventure and high position.

He applied and was rejected. He applied again, and this second application was accepted. He became third officer, or fourth in the line of command, since the expedition was organized along Navy lines and in fact operated almost as a unit of the Navy.

The official explanation for the turnabout was that Shackleton's experience with canvas would be of value—the *Discovery* was to be sailed to Antarctica in order to save fuel—for the Navy, unlike the merchant marine, did not require an apprenticeship in sail; but undoubtedly his friend's father, that rich patron, had something to do with it.

Shackleton knew nothing of any science. He had never visited a polar region. He had never even seen a pair of skis or a dog sled. But after all, as much could be said of virtually every other man on the expedition. Shackleton was young, and that was the main thing. They were all young. "The Babes in the Wood," the papers called them, referring to the fact that the specially stressed *Discovery* was made of that material.

Loudly cheered, and with all flags flapping, they sailed from Spithead on August 5th, 1901.

A year and a half later, Ernest Henry Shackleton came back alone, a bitter man.

CHAPTER 4

HE MIGHT have thought that he had been discriminated against as a non-Navy man (they had wangled a sub-lieutenant's commission for him, but this was only a temporary thing and anyway it was in the Reserve, and regular Navy men looked upon Reservists much as Army men looked on members of the militia) but he did not let this feeling show. He remained loyal to the expedition which like all polar expeditions had a continuing need for funds. He was elected a member of the Royal Geographical Society, which made much of him. He lectured, using lantern slides made from photographs he himself had taken.

As a lecturer, though without any previous experience, he was a tremendous success. He was a natural storyteller, and a straight talker, one you could trust. He had an easy, relaxed, Irish charm and a merry smile. His dark brown hair was neatly parted in the middle. His notes were always in order; he never knew stage fright; and there wasn't a pompous bone in his body.

All of this was not making a place for himself. It was not enabling him to marry Emily. The fees for the lectures he turned over to the expedition, and he spent much time, too, in giving that organization the benefit of his experience when a new relief ship was outfitted. He was always openhanded, even to the point of extravagance.

His brilliance as a speaker seems rather to have startled him, and at one time he thought to cash in on it by forming an international lecture bureau with himself as the chief attraction. Like all of his plans this one was grandiose, and like most of them it fell through.

Of one thing he was sure: He wasn't going back to the merchant marine to wait interminable years for his seniors to die. That was kid stuff, and here he was edging 30.

He did apply for a commission in the regular Navy, but was informed that there were none open. This is just as well. He never could have endured the discipline.

Unexpectedly he got himself a sub-editor's post with *The Royal Magazino.* He had never before been in an editorial office, and his command of written English, as distinguished from spoken English, was limited, to say the least. He enjoyed this job, though he did not last long at it.

The Royal Scottish Geographical Society—not to be confused with the Royal Geographical Society, which was English, and of which Shackleton was a more or less honorary member, was in need of a new secretary. The pay would be about the same as that in his editorial post, but the dignity would be greater. He applied formally and forcefully. The Scots were in no hurry. They hemmed and hawed, while he chafed. At last they accepted him.

He plunged into the work. He scandalized the stuffy members by installing a telephone in his office—and even, God help us, a typewriter. But he did increase the membership and greatly better the Society's financial position. Also, he popularized the lecture circuit, giving many of the lectures himself. Robert Falcon Scott returned from the bottom of the world at just about this time, and Shackleton was able to talk him into appearing several times for the benefit of the Society, in Edinburgh, Glasgow, and Aberdeen.

He and Emily were married in Christ Church, Westminster, on April 9th, 1904. They postponed their honeymoon because he was so busy. They moved into a house that he had rented, remodeled, redecorated, and staffed, at No. 14, South Learmonth Gardens, on the outskirts of Edinburgh.

Yet already he was yawning. He had hoped that Edinburgh and his new post there would prove the place he sought, the position, whereas, he realized, they might have been lost in London. He was not really disappointed in the Scottish capital, but the challenge was not enough to keep him occupied, and soon he was seeking work—and wealth—elsewhere.

Idleness was something that he never submitted to.

At one time he was all afizz about a plan to supply the Russian government with chartered ships in which to evacuate her armies from the Far East at the end of the Russo-Japanese War. This would mean a profit of £100,000, he told Emily. The plan blew up.

He started to promote Tabard Cigarettes. Shackleton himself did not smoke, but he could not deny that the habit was growing all around him, and Tabard should go over big, very big. In fact it was moderately successful, but only moderately, and he soon lost interest in it.

Moderation was not for him.

He and one of his brothers-in-law, a professor, made elaborate plans to found an international news agency. The agency somehow never came into being.

He took up golf, his wife's favorite diversion, but he never became as expert as she was. He pressed too hard, and he could not develop a smooth follow-through.

There was a knight named William Beardmore (he later became Lord Invernairn), who had extensive interests in both England and Scotland—big things like railroads and shipyards, things that would catch the Shackletonian imagination—and he took a liking to the young secretary of the Royal Scottish Geographical Society. Just what he expected to do with this newcomer to his staff—for Shackleton was given a regular job, at £300 a year—is not clear. It is certain, however, that Shackleton himself, afire with enthusiasm, was led to believe, perhaps by Lady Beardmore, who feared for her husband's health, that he would soon be in charge of the whole industrial empire; and when it became evident that for the present at least he was being used only as an arranger of meetings and conferences, an organizer, a sort of glorified *maitre d'hôtel*, he shuffled off.

The doddering members of the Royal Scottish Geographical Society suffered all this as best they could, for undeniably, they told themselves, the lad had done a good piece of work in his brusque way; but when he ventured into politics many a head was shaken, many a tongue clicked, and though Shackleton was not literally asked to resign it was made patent to him that he would be asked soon.

He knew nothing about politics, but this did not deter him, and when he was asked to stand for Parliament as a Liberal-Unionist candidate from Dundee he accepted with suspicious alacrity. He conducted a slashing campaign, and was especially notable in the clinches, when heckled, for he loved a good fight. The crowds cheered him. But they voted for the other fellow. Shackleton was snowed under.

No matter. The Beardmore connection, if it did not end by making him a mogul, did give him access to many men of great wealth, and at the time when he severed relations with the Geographical Society he had already stashed away a large number of promises and pledges, and was willing at last to disclose his real plans. Steamships, cigarettes, railways, the House of Commons

—these could no longer divert his attention from his overall aim.

Yes, he announced, he was about to make another dash for the South Pole. And this time he would get there.

CHAPTER 5

THE FIRST consideration, as it was always to be, was money. The two learned societies that had helped to back Scott had nothing left. The Navy wasn't interested. There was no fund and no official sponsorship behind this venture, which was to be made on credit, a one-man show, deriving all of its force, all of its steam, from the personality of Ernest Henry Shackleton.

He was ebullient, imperishably optimistic—or he seemed to be. He was learning—and if he was abashed to learn it, he did not let this show—that he who would lead a polar expedition must first of all collect funds. He threw himself into this business.

He had rather liked lecturing just at first, but he had come to look upon it as a chore. Nevertheless, he lectured extensively, and he was quick to point out that his fees would be much higher and his engagements more numerous once he had discovered the South Pole. He counted upon this. He urged it as an argument, a piece of credit, when he asked for loans. This and the book he would inevitably write could be viewed as guarantees of repayment, as collateral.

His first rosy prospectus called for a small ship, which would not be used as a camp, merely as a means of transportation, and only ten men, including the chief. These men would do everything, the sailors learning something about science on the way south, as Shackleton himself had done in the *Discovery,* while the scientists would be expected to handle sail, hold the helm, and perhaps even shovel coal. There would be no ranks, except as needed for the administration of the ship. Nobody would call anybody else "sir."

That ship, he estimated, would cost £7,000, while the rest of the expedition—wages, supplies, equipment, everything—would require another £10,000. He was out to raise the £17,000 and then he would go. It was an amazingly naive figure, but there is reason to think that Shackleton himself believed it—at first.

He was rocked back on his heels when he started asking old *Discovery* chums to join him and learned from at least two of them, Dr. Wilson of the dash, and Lieutenant George Mulock, the regular Navy man who had replaced Shackleton himself, that though they thanked him for asking, they had to decline because they had already promised Robert Falcon Scott to go with *him*.

It was the first time Shackleton had heard that Scott was planning another expedition; and, using Wilson as a sort of corresponding go-between, he got in touch with his former chief, who was at sea.

Like a couple of wary swordsmen they circled one another at a distance, each afraid to close the measure. Scott could be a formidable foe, if foe he had to be. His prestige was prodigious, whereas Shackleton was virtually unknown.

Yes, Scott said stiffly, he was preparing another expedition, but he had not made public announcement of this fact because he shunned the publicity that would ensue: it might mar his plans, he said. In any event it would take him two years, maybe three, to get ready to go. He meant to use the same base on McMurdo Sound. Surely Shackleton did not contemplate the use of McMurdo Sound? No, Shackleton thought rather to base somewhere in Edward VII Land, east of the Ross Ice Barrier as McMurdo Sound was west of it, but if he could not find the right place there, a little nearer to the Pole than McMurdo Sound, he did not see why he couldn't use Scott's previous base, which no doubt remained in good condition.

Scott, inexplicably, was shocked. He cried out that he had been betrayed. He appealed to Dr. Wilson.

Shackleton was confused, as well he might be. He knew that Scott was a highly emotional man, an introvert whom he never had been able to understand, but he could see no justification for these shrill cries of anguish. The building on McMurdo Sound was not Scott's personal property; it had been built on public funds. Nor was the Sound itself Scott's indisputable domain. He hadn't discovered it; another Navy captain (for

Scott had been promoted since his return from Antarctica), Ross, had done that more than half a century ago. Why shouldn't Shackleton use the place? He too appealed to Dr. Billy Wilson.

Gently, that gentle man pointed out that "the gilt will be off the gingerbread" if Shackleton happened to discover the South Pole out of a plant established by his former leader, who was himself preparing to do the same thing. It would be like riding to glory on another man's coat tails, though the good doctor did not put it that way. The public would disapprove. And what Ernest Henry Shackleton needed most of all was the good will of the public, was it not?

Now Shackleton saw the point. It was preposterous that two men should haggle over the distribution of a vast, icy, unexplored stretch of land on the other side of the world, a land that was not even claimed by their country—though it was claimed by New Zealand, directly north of it, an ideal jumping-off point. Scott had no right to make such a demand, and Shackleton had no obligation to heed him. But heed him Shackleton did, for Dr. Wilson was right. The public wouldn't enjoy the looks of the business. And for all the talk about scientific aims that Shackleton used when he appealed for funds, it was the discovery of the South Pole that was uppermost in his mind. Only by being the first man to reach 90 degrees south could he prove himself to be worthy of Emily.

So he submitted. He even made a solemn pledge in writing that he would not venture west of 170 west, a line of longitude that bisects the vast Ross Ice Shelf. It was a very stupid thing to do.

This matter settled, he turned to more specific preparations. He put out another prospectus, somewhat enlarging his original modest plan and allowing for the use of some dogs, animals he had previously been opposed to. Nine of these, descendants of the Siberian dogs used in the *Southern Cross* expedition of 1898-1900, would be purchased from a breeder in Stewart Island, New Zealand. Shackleton also arranged to have the Hongkong and Shanghai bank send an experienced man to Tientsin to buy 15 Siberian ponies, which were to be sent to New Zealand by way of Australia. He had at this time great faith in ponies, which had been used in the Arctic. A pony could drag 1,800 pounds on a sledge, though it required ten pounds of food a day. A dog could drag only 100 pounds, but needed only one and a half pounds of food, while a man, who needed two pounds of food a day in ordinary circumstances, could drag a 200-pound load. But Shackleton's experience with dogs had not been a happy one.

He proposed also to take an automobile, if somebody would donate one; somebody promptly did. This caused a stir among the journalists as, no doubt, it was meant to do.

He hired an agent and opened offices at 9 Regent Street, Waterloo Place, under the name of the British Antarctic Expedition.

Since he wasn't to be permitted to use Scott's hut, he had one of his own built in sections. It was to measure 33 by 19 by 8 feet on the outside—not palatial, but big enough to sleep twelve men. It was to be made of fir. He bought no furniture, for he believed that the Venesta wooden packing cases of food that he had ordered could be converted, one by one, as they were emptied. This was a good idea.

He went to Norway to order other pieces of equipment—ten twelve-foot sledges for the ponies to pull, 18 eleven-foot sledges for the men, two seven-foot sledges for the dogs, many wolfskin mittens, a large supply of finnskoes, or shoes made of reindeer hide, and 15 sleeping bags. Twelve of the sleeping bags were individual ones, the other three being three-man bags to be used only by far-flung exploring parties when the weather was at its bitterest, the idea being that the men would keep one another warm. Shackleton believed that some semblance of privacy under ordinary conditions would help morale.

He studied a great deal about the comfort and well-being of his men, too, when he bought food supplies. He demanded not only plenty, but variety, for he knew that eating the same thing day after day for weeks or even months could sap the strength of anybody. He was determined that there would not be even a passing brush of scurvy on this expedition.

He was disappointed, at first, in his vessel. He had hoped to buy the *Bjorn,* a wooden ship built especially for Arctic work, in Norway; but she proved too expensive for him. He settled for a vessel he had never seen, only heard about, the 200-ton *Nimrod,* a sealer from Newfoundland. His heart plummeted when he looked at her for the first time in the Thames. She was disgracefully dumpy, anything but picturesque. Her masts were rotten. Her decks were dirty, and she was rancid with seal oil all through, an abomination to the nose. Her sleazy sails were not good enough for his purposes. But he went right to work on her, and in time, thanks to his expert supervision, she was turned into a taut, trim, even trig craft, so that he came to be positively proud of her.

The care and fussy attention he had given to the purchase of equipment and food no longer seemed to be with him when he started to select the most important items of all—the men. Here he had his own method, which was purely intuitive.

Not all of the *Discovery* veterans he had approached turned him down. Frank Wild and Ernest Joyce, both regular Navy men but willing to resign, signed up for the *Nimrod* undertaking. Together with him, they were the only ones who had ever visited a polar region. Wild, a slight, quick-grinning pipe smoker, in which Shackleton had great faith, was to be second in command. He and Joyce were petty officers first class.

Others were chosen, it would seem, almost by whim. One recalled afterward that Shackleton, having studied him briefly, asked if he could sing, and when he started to protest cut it off with, "Oh, I don't mean that Caruso stuff. I just mean can you sing with the boys now and then over a beer?" *That* kind of music, the applicant replied, he could make; and he was hired on the spot.

Another was startled when Shackleton asked him if he could recognize gold in the ground. He would not have been, if he had known Shackleton better. Shackleton's irrepressible romanticism included a small boy's belief in treasure, preferably buried; he was always hoping that he would stumble over a cache of uncut diamonds. Once he almost invested in one of the many companies that have dug up Cocos Island in the Galapagos time after time in the past hundred years or so without ever finding a centavo of the treasure some pirates were supposed to have buried there. He was saved from this investment because he didn't have any money.

The applicant answered no, he wouldn't know gold in its raw form. He got the job anyway. Shackleton liked his looks.

They were mostly young men, and the youngest of all was Sir Philip Brocklehurst who was 19. The reason for his signing up, once he had expressed an eagerness to go, was obvious: His mother was a large contributor to the cause. Shackleton might well have taken him anyway, for Sir Philip was the sort of lad he liked, fast with his fists, a promising Cambridge lightweight. Shackleton agreed that he could be one of the small party of men who would make the ultimate dash.

(Though the South Magnetic Pole was one of the spots aimed at and the most important one from a scientific point of view, the "ultimate dash" was always taken to mean the dash for the South Pole, the geographical pole.

At last they were ready, and they steamed out of the Thames at a brisk six knots. The Admiralty had ordered them to stop at Cowes, and there they received a really glittering sendoff, one worthy of Scott himself. Shackleton, unlike Scott, was not chary of publicity, and he still owed a great deal of money.

Not only did the King come aboard at Cowes, but he brought the Queen with him, and also the Prince of Wales, Princess Victoria, the Duke of Connaught, and sundry other royal personages, who obligingly smiled, shook hands, and posed for pictures. It was a glorious occasion. Afterward the *Nimrod*, all flags flying, smoke billowing from her stubby stack, turned south. She was off.

CHAPTER 6

NOW, what manner of land is this that though bleak and bare, gusty, treacherous, murderously cold, and appallingly uncomfortable could lure men from the other side of the world to come and taste its terrors? What is Antarctica's appeal?

It is uninhabited by man or beast. It could offer no fields or forests, no vegetation of any kind. It is subject, the year round, to savage storms, blizzards that sprang up suddenly and blotted out every sight, so that a man could scarcely see his own legs and could readily be lost ten feet from a tent; and these blizzards might blow with unabated fury for days on end, even for weeks.

Two-hundred-mile-an-hour gales are not uncommon. These would make any Caribbean hurricane seem a zephyr. It is the highest continent. The South Pole itself, though set in a depression in the middle of the world's largest plateau, is two miles above sea level. With 5,000,000 square miles, it is the fifth largest continent, twice as big as Australia, almost as big as South America, about the size of the United States and Mexico put together.

It is the coldest continent—much colder than the Arctic. There are two reasons for this. One is that the Antarctic is so high, perched, you might say, on a series of mountains. The other is that while the territory around the North Pole is ice and snow on top of water, Antarctica under all that snow and ice is solid land, most of it rock, which holds the cold and even, in a manner of speaking, reflects it. Special thermometers have to be made to register the temperatures of Antarctica. (Vostok, the permanent Russian base, in August of 1960 reported a reading of 126 degrees below zero Fahrenheit.) Yet there is reason to think that in the age of dinosaurs, long before man, it was tropical.

Besides the mountain ranges, Antarctica is stippled and crisscrossed by many glaciers, most of them much bigger than any others on earth. (The Beardmore Glacier, which Shackleton was to discover and to name after his benefactor, is wider than the famous Aletsch of Switzerland is long.) These contain, in frozen form, more water than there is in all the rivers and brooks and creeks of all the rest of the world. If the glaciers and the snow—Antarctica has 90 to 95 percent of all the snow in the world—were suddenly to melt, it would raise the level of all the oceans by at least 200 feet and move the Atlantic coast of the United States back to western Pennsylvania.

The Antarctic Ocean, which completely surrounds Antarctica—South America is 850 miles away, Australia 1,800 miles, the southern tip of Africa 2,400 miles—is in everything except temperature a jungle. It teems with life, from micro-scopic plankton to the biggest whales.

The whales of Antarctica, incidentally, spout not water but steam. An even more curious sight is men "breathing rainbows" as they talk to one another when the sun is out. The breath, that is, in the intense cold is instantly frozen into the form of tiny ice particles, each a prism, each separately shining with all the colors of the spec-trum.

But then, Antarctica, though poor in many re-spects, is rich in optical illusions, brought about by the sun, the ice, the snow, and the utter ab-sence from the air of any dust. Fata morgana and blue St. Elmo's fire are common occurrences. The sunsets are green, and sometimes the sun seems to set three or four times, and the moon rises the same way, as though they can't make up their minds. The atmospheric phenomenon called ice blink causes objects near or far, the man standing next to you, a mountain many miles distant, to disappear, then come back, then disappear again, and come back again. . . . The aurora aus-tralis is perhaps a shade less gaudy than the cel-ebrated aurora borealis of the Arctic, being eerier and more yellow, but it is a sensational sight all the same. Mirages are frequent—and not stingy little Sahara mirages but real, full, long-distance ones. Men on the shore of Antarctica have seen relief ships in the sky long before any ship was visible on the horizon. When these are upside down, there is no doubt that they are mirages; but sometimes they are right side up. Whales can be seen the same way, right side up as well as upside down.

It is this trickiness of light, together with the fact that bergs and ice floes make it difficult even to approach Antarctica for a better look, that caused so many of the early explorers to report the presence of things that weren't there at all. Every officer on a given ship, for example, might swear that he had seen a certain mountain at a certain point along the coast, when what he had in fact seen was the reflection of that mountain, which itself might be fifty miles or more away. This made for perplexity, not to mention cries of "liar!"

Though it had been discovered, or at any rate first sighted, less than a hundred years before— by whom has been a matter of dispute ever since (see Appendix A)—the existence of Antarctica had been known since ancient times. It is a mistake to think that before Columbus everybody thought the world was flat. Men who were interested always knew that it was round and that it turned on its axis; and it stood to reason, these men argued, that there must be a large land mass in the Southern Hemisphere to counterbalance the large land mass that they had seen with their own eyes in the Northern Hemisphere, for otherwise wouldn't the world wobble? (It does wobble a bit, really, which is why the South Pole, like the North Pole, never stays long in one place.)

The southern waters have always had a bad name among mariners. Maybe there *was* a big island or even a continent down there, but what of it? Who would want to go to such a place, anyway?

Now and then some ship might be blown far off course while rounding the Horn, and on its return the skipper would vow that he had seen land at such-and-such a degree of south latitude, but the records are unreliable, and it could be that these were just islands. It was not until the time of James Cook that anybody made a deliberate attempt to go as far south as possible.

Cook's first round-the-world voyage was for the purpose of marking the passage of Venus from a point in Tahiti, today called Venus Point, but he had sealed orders to explore to the south after this task had been completed. He examined the group of which Tahiti is one, naming it the Society Islands after the Royal Society that had sent him out. He explored the North and South islands of New Zealand and the strait between them, since named after him, and established that New Zealand at least was not part of any great southern land mass. He carefully explored the east coast of Australia. He confirmed that New Guinea, too, could not possibly be a part of any far-south continent.

On his second voyage, he was under orders to look hard for that perhaps mythical continent, and he did so to the best of his ability, which was very great. He passed the Antarctic Circle, the first man to do so, January 16, 1773. He recrossed it several times, searching with zeal, but always being forced back by the huge masses of floating ice, and though he discovered and named many

41

islands he never did sight Antarctica. The highest latitude he ever reached was 67 degrees 31 minutes, or about 1,000 miles from the South Pole.

James Cook, the son of a Yorkshire farm laborer, did as much for geography as any man who ever lived, but in the case of the search for Antarctica it is to be feared that he discouraged it, for when he returned from that second voyage it was to report that he didn't believe such a land mass existed. If a man of the caliber of Cook couldn't find it, popular opinion went, then it just wasn't there.

Sealers in the early years of the Nineteenth Century, some English, others American, most of the latter being from Stonington, Connecticut, discovered and to some extent explored sundry islands in the wild sea between Antarctica and the southern tip of South America, Tierra del Fuego, and one of these might have been the first to sight the mainland (see Appendix A). However, these men were interested in slaughtering seals for their fur, not in penning valuable records, and when the seals had been wiped out— hundreds of thousands of them within a few years—the sealers went away, leaving nothing.

Captain—later Admiral—Fabian Thaddeus Thaddovich von Bellinghausen was a German navigator sent to southern polar parts by the Czar of Russia. He had two well-equipped vessels, and he took his time, for he was an exceedingly careful man. For three years he zigzagged back and forth across the Antarctic Circle, keeping as far south as he conveniently could. He made many discoveries, and he might have sighted the mainland—there are those who think that he did—but he never claimed to have done so.

There had been subsequent commercial accidental voyages of discovery around the edges of Antarctica and several official government ventures, notable among the latter being those of Wilkes the American and Ross the Englishman, but these were no more than shore chartings. Antarctica was not easy to reach. Because of the ice flocs, seamen might get within a few miles of it and never be able to land. Until Scott, with his scouting party on skis, there had been no determined attempt to explore the interior.

This, then, was the continent that Ernest Henry Shackleton proposed to conquer.

CHAPTER 7

AT BEGGING, which was, of course, the biggest part of the business, Shackleton had been only moderately successful. He had gotten the show on the road, but he was by no means sure of keeping it there. Reserve funds were lacking for wages, additional supplies, emergencies. Shackleton himself was not aboard the *Nimrod* when she steamed away from Cowes. It would be a long, slow trip, by way of the Cape of Good Hope, the whole Indian Ocean, and half of the Pacific Ocean, to New Zealand, and the leader still had some unfinished business to take care of. When at last he did leave, it was to cross the Channel, and to go by train to Paris and then Marseilles, where he boarded a much faster vessel that would take him to Australia by way of the Suez Canal and the Red Sea. He made friends easily, and he made many friends on this voyage, some of whom even contributed cash to the expedition.

In Australia and later in New Zealand, Shackleton did a great deal of lecturing, and he drew enthusiastic crowds. Impetuous as always, he donated his fees to local charities. However, the

Commonwealth of Australia voted to contribute £5,000 to the fund, and the government of New Zealand contributed another £1,000.

Despite the drain on his resources, he increased his scientific staff in Australia. A physicist, Douglas Mawson, an expert in minerology and petrology—after all, Shackleton still had that fondness for buried or at least underground treasure, and Antarctica might just have valuable mineral deposits, if a man could get to them—joined up from Adelaide University; and from Sydney came Professor T.W.E. David, a merry little geologist, who was almost 50 but wiry and untiring, a man, moreover, who in Shackleton's own felicitous phrase, "could charm a bird off a bough."

The dogs, a snappish lot, were brought from Stewart Island, the ponies from Quail Island, where they had been set down to graze. These were lodged in small wooden houses and in wooden stalls on deck. The stalls were promptly named the Cavalry Club, and professors, among others, kept them shoveled out.

What with all the animals, supplies, and coal, it became clear that the *Nimrod,* before she started, was seriously overloaded: there were only a few feet of freeboard. Unless they were lucky with the wind and could make the whole voyage under sail, which was too much to count upon, they would use up so much fuel on the trip south that there would be barely enough to get the *Nimrod* back to New Zealand, none at all to leave with the party that was prepared to spend the long Antarctic night on land. Shackleton had estimated that he would need a minimum of 30 tons for this alone.

Why Shackleton had not provided against this is not clear, but seemingly it had not occurred to him, and now he was faced with a major problem. He soon solved it. The Union Steamship Company offered to charter him a tow ship, a small steamer called *Koonya,* and the president of the company paid half the cost out of his own pocket, while the New Zealand government paid the other half.

New Year's Day of 1908, at four o'clock in the afternoon, they pulled—or rather *were* pulled—out of Lyttleton.

At once they were hit by the worst storm any of them had ever known. It lasted almost two weeks, and though sometimes it was worse than at other times, it was always bad. Gear and equipment not yet properly stowed were thrown everywhere. The pumps were worked night and day. The animals panicked, and two of the ponies, Zulu and Doctor, were so badly battered that they had to be shot. Sleep was confined to short snatches. Yet the spirits of the men remained high. Shackleton, on the bridge almost continuously, grinned at one sailor who, ordered to reassemble the contents of a smashed crate of potatoes, went about the job on a heaving, wet deck, gayly warbling, "Here we go gathering nuts in May!" Several times it was feared that they'd have to let go of the towline, a nine-ton chain-and-hemp connector; but they fought it out, both skippers doing a wonderful job. On January 13th the fury subsided, and they were granted a chance to get dry.

The agreement was that the *Koonya* would keep pulling until the first pack ice was encountered, and it was January 15th when the towline was reeled in. The little leading vessel had established two records: she had towed farther, 1,510 miles, than any other vessel not built for that purpose, and she was the first steel vessel to go beyond the Antarctic Circle.

She transferred a lot of fresh meat, the gift of generous New Zealanders, to the *Nimrod,* which in turn transferred to the *Koonya* part of the 24,000 stamps specially struck off for this occasion. This had been another stunt to raise money. Shackleton himself had been duly sworn in as a New Zealand postmaster. Other stamps were to go back on the *Nimrod.* Still others, God knows why, were to be buried in a brass tube in the snows of Antarctica.

The *Koonya* circled the *Nimrod* once, and then steamed off north. They were left alone.

January 23rd the vast Ross Ice Shelf was sighted. They cruised along this for some time, looking for Balloon Inlet where, in 1902, on the first landing from the *Discovery,* Scott and then Shackleton, singly, had ascended in a captive balloon to see what they could see on the other side of the ice shelf, a prodigious feat when it is remembered that neither had ever been up in the air before.

Balloon Inlet simply wasn't there. Shackleton was sure of his navigation, and he would remember the place, but it had disappeared.

This is not as strange as it might seem. From time to time huge masses of ice, a million tons and more, inexplicably break off from the ice shelf and plop, splashing and hissing, into the sea to float off as icebergs. This process, called "calving," sometimes is heralded by preliminary cracks like mortar fire. Any vessel near at hand would, of course, be squashed. It is well not to sail too close to the Ross Ice Shelf.

They turned east, hoping to find a place to land and to camp on Edward VII Land, but the ice would not permit this. Every lead they ventured into threatened to close around them, giving them barely time to scamper for safety.

And time was pressing. The skipper was worried about his supply of coal. He reckoned that he would need 110 tons of it to get back to New Zealand, besides the 30 tons Shackleton wanted. He kept urging Shackleton to turn west and settle for McMurdo Sound, which they both knew.

Shackleton was technically the owner of the *Nimrod,* and he had his own master's certificate, but this did not make him the captain. The captain hired for the occasion was R. G. England, who had been the chief officer of the *Discovery's* relief ship, *Morning,* and so was familiar with these waters and knew what ice could do if it was not treated with respect. There were those among the men who contended that Captain England treated it with too much respect, and it could be that Shackleton also came to feel that way.

Others urged Shackleton to turn toward McMurdo Sound. If he didn't, they might get caught in the ice and have to spend the whole winter there, not just the landing party but the ship and everybody in it. Or, what could be worse, in a little while they might not be able to get close enough to land at all, and be obliged to make a humiliating retreat to New Zealand.

At last he sighed and gave in. The *Nimrod* was turned west. It was a painful decision for Shackleton, for he had promised Scott he would not do this and he believed it would cost him, among other things, the friendship of Dr. Wilson, as indeed it did. But it was the only way he could save his expedition. Scott himself, in the circumstances, probably would have done the same thing.

They tried to reach Hut Point, where Scott's camp had been, but again the ice said no. The nearest they could get was Cape Royds, named after the first officer of the *Discovery*, about 20 miles away, and they viewed it through a glass from the crow's-nest. It looked in excellent condition. Things do not rot or rust in Antarctica, where there are no germs. The hut might have been blown away or buried in snow, but there it was.

They had 180 tons of stores, besides the coal. Once put on the ice alongside the vessel, these stores must be immediately hauled to more solid ground a mile or more away, lest the ice split away and float off with them. It was back-breaking work, made worse on occasion by Captain England's reluctance to risk his ship. Many times he backed away, causing a stoppage in the work, and once he stayed away for four days. The men didn't like it. But at last, on February 22nd, all was ready. The men scrawled hasty, last-minute letters. Shackleton wrote to Emily:

"Goodbye Darling wife. God keep you and our children. I think we will get the Pole. I cannot write more. My whole heart is with you.

Your husband
Ernest.

P.S. "I am fit and well"

The *Nimrod* sailed north. The men finished assembling the shack. They built themselves cubicles inside it, each for two men. They stabled the ponies and the dogs. They made everything fast. They set up weather instruments and a laboratory. One party on skis visited Scott's hut and learned that it was indeed marvelously well preserved. With a view to having future fresh meat, they slaughtered 129 penguins that had ventured too close, and they stashed the bodies under the snow in a well-marked spot. Ordinarily these could have been left on the surface, since all Antarctica is one great deep-freeze, but the dogs, maddened by the smell, set up a horrid yammering, so the bodies were concealed. They held a church service, and sang "Onward, Christian Soldiers." Two of the bitches had litters of puppies. And so the long dim polar winter set in.

CHAPTER 8

GEORGE MARSTON, the artist of the expedition, like most of the others was young. But unlike most of the others, he was large, a great sheepdog of a person. He shared with the Boss a fondness for practical jokes—Shackleton was always called the Boss, the only title used in that camp except that David was called the Professor. Marston was called, for no apparent reason, Putty.

Marston lived in a 6-by-7-foot cubicle with Bernard Day, who was in charge of the automobile. Like the others—for the cubicles were uniform—it had one real wall, the wooden, outside one, and three walls that consisted only of burlap sacking separating it from other cubicles on either side and from the main eating room in front. These berths had playful names—No. I Park Lane, The Old Curiosity Shop, Rogues' Retreat. The Day-Marston cubicle was called The Gables. On the real wall, Marston painted a fireplace complete with mantel on which was a jarful of roses. In the grate he painted a roaring fire. It was very cozy, very realistic, and the other men often asked permission to look at it. It made them feel warm, they said.

The real warmth, such as it was, was supplied by a large potbellied cooking stove in the middle of the main room. It smoked, and the place soon was sooty, and so were the men, a condition that grew worse as the winter wore on.

Otherwise they were not uncomfortable. The worst part of Antarctic winter, the dark and appallingly cold part, lasts about four months. The greatest danger, of course, was boredom. They had been picked, in part, with this in mind. They were variegated but determinedly amiable. Seldom was there so much as a smitch of snarling.

At any excuse, such as a birthday, they would stage a feast; and in addition they had informal songfests, mock trials, lectures, a contest to see who was the worst singer (the Boss won this), dog derbies, haircutting parties, and the like. It was all great fun.

Before the full onset of winter, though well after the supply ship had departed, six of them, including the Professor, whose 50th birthday they had just celebrated, climbed Mount Erebus, a nearby active volcano more than 13,000 feet tall— and they started from sea level. Except for the fact that Sir Philip Brocklehurst got his feet frozen so that Dr. Marshall had to amputate a couple of his toes afterward, the party was a complete success.

Shackleton had planned to visit the penguin rookery at Cape Crozier to study the birds' mating and nesting habits, and with this in mind he

53

had brought along a movie camera and a phonograph recorder; but because of the nature of the ice, this proved to be impossible.

They had also brought with them a printing press, and while they did not get out a regular journal as the much larger *Discovery* party had done, with Shackleton as editor until he was sent back to England, they did assemble a series of poems, comic skits, and excellent articles and lectures, not to mention art work, which would make a wonderful souvenir. It was called aurora australis.

The automobile proved to be of almost no use. The wheels, whether wooden or equipped with rubber tires—both kinds were tried—would sink into the snow. On ice it behaved better, so long as the ice was level, and it could carry large loads, larger than a sledge could carry, at speeds up to 15 miles an hour; but as soon as the surface sloped, its wheels would whirl helplessly, getting no grip. It gave them a lot of trouble to start, too, and the carburetor was temperamental.

Another drawback was that the automobile could not get over a snow-bridged crevasse. These crevasses were jagged slits in the ice, maybe a few inches wide, maybe many yards, and some of them seemed to have no bottom. Many were covered with snow, and so could not be seen from above. A dog sled, even a pony, followed by a man on skis, might easily go over such a bridge and never know it, but an automobile would be sure to disappear. There were none of those crevasses near the base camp, but as

Shackleton had reason to know, there were many of them on the route that stretched toward the South Pole. Still, nobody even dreamed of taking the automobile to the South Pole anyway.

The dogs were well berthed in wooden houses that the men called "dogloos," though the Eskimo practice of building shelters of block ice never had been practiced in Antarctica. The dogs were quarrelsome beasts, as Scott's had been, always fighting among themselves; but they were readily trained. A great fuss was made about the puppies.

The ponies, like the dogs, were supplied with wooden houses just outside the hut. Here the explorers had bad luck. Of the original 15 ponies, six had not survived the long trip to New Zealand; the tropics were too much for them. Two more had been destroyed as a result of the storm between New Zealand and Antarctica. That left seven, and now, suddenly, one after the other, three of these died.

Autopsies showed that death was caused by a toxic sand, a sort of volcanic sand, which they had found on a nearby beach and probably had eaten as a substitute for salt. One of them, ironically, had been named Sandy. The other four, Quan, Grisi, Socks, and Chinaman, did not seem to be affected, but thereafter they were denied beach privileges.

Come the spring, there were to be three sledging parties, the western, the northern, and the southern, and only two men would remain at the hut, reading instruments around the clock.

The western party would visit the mountains in the western part of the continent, and was later to hook up with the northern party. It contained the two youngest men on the expedition, Brocklehurst the baronet and Raymond Priestly, a geologist, who was instructed to keep a sharp lookout for possible gems. It was led by an Australian, Bertram Armytage.

The northern party was to go to the South Magnetic Pole, never before visited, though it had been located from afar. This was strictly a scientific group, consisting of David, Mawson, and Dr. Alistair Forbes Mackay.

It was around the southern party, as it was always called, the dash party, as it was thought of, that most of the interest centered. Partly because of the cutting off of Brocklehurst's toes and partly because of the death of the three Siberian ponies, Shackleton decided to pare this down from the six originally planned to four.

Sir Philip was debarred because of his foot. Dr. Marshall, after a careful examination of Ernest Joyce, reported that he detected a faint heart murmur, so Joyce too was dropped. They would go with the western party.

The South Pole party, then, was to consist of the Boss, Frank Wild, that small but seemingly indestructible second-in-command, Dr. Eric Marshall, and Jameson Boyd Adams, who like Shackleton had been a merchant marine officer.

When their work was finished, all three parties were to assemble at the base camp on Cape Royds on or before February 25th, there to board the relief ship *Nimrod*. Shackleton was careful to instruct the man in charge of that camp in his absence, James Murray, the second-oldest member of the expedition, that if the southern party had not returned by March 1st he was given permission to postpone the departure of the *Nimrod*—provided the new skipper of the *Nimrod* (for it had been understood when he left that Captain England would resign) concurred—until March 10th. On no account was the *Nimrod* to stay longer than that. If it was to sail without the members of the southern party, Murray should post three volunteers, equipped with sledges and dogs and food for seven men for one year, at the base camp, in the faint hope that the missing ones would somehow find their way in.

He was very careful about it. Each man got his individual instructions, in writing, and every possible contingency had been foreseen, including, of course, that of his own death.

In a last-minute surprise move, he raised all their wages. However, he had to tack a proviso to that. Their wages were to be raised if, when all accounts were in, the expedition had any money left—in other words, *if* they had discovered the South Pole.

The western party went forth, and then the northern party. On October 29th, 1908, with only two men to wave it goodbye, the southern party set forth. It was a beautiful morning.

CHAPTER 9

ACTUALLY, their jumping-off place was Hut Point, Scott's old camp, which Shackleton had equipped with a stove and used as a way station, stocking it with forward foods: three men had been pinned there once for five days in a blizzard. It was 20 miles nearer the Pole than was the camp at Cape Royds. There was no reason why Shackleton should not use this building. He left it in better condition than he found it.

Their car, an Arrol-Johnston, was used in this early shove, and it was reasonably effective on the level ice, before the Ross Ice Shelf was reached. It was not a truck or a lorry, only a chassis, for it was not meant to carry supplies but to drag them. At the beginning of the dash it was used primarily to give the ponies a chance to conserve their strength.

The ponies were a problem. Grisi, at the very first camp, kicked Adams in the leg just below the knee so hard that the bone was laid open. Quan was always chewing through its harness. And Socks went lame within the first hour. They were willing beasts, but like the dogs they had to be watched.

Also with the idea of conserving the strength of the ponies, the dogs had been used in the preliminary work of establishing a depot at Minna's Bluff, 120 miles south of Cape Royds.

The party left from base October 29th, five calender days before the Scott party had started its 1902 dash, but there was more to be done— again because of the ponies. The ponies were to be fed a concoction of maize, some stuff called Maujee ration, and compressed fodder brought from Australia. The maize had to be freshly ground, and a large supply of it, together with a mill, had been deposited in the *Discovery* hut. Because of the work of grinding, at which they took turns, and also in order to allow Socks to get back full use of its lame leg, the party spent several days at Scott's former hut, and it was not until November 3rd that it made its real start.

Shackleton, who customarily kept his nerves under control, was edgy and snappish during this delay at the *Discovery* hut, but once they got under way he quieted down.

On November 5th and 6th there was a heavy snow, so that they could not see where they were going and had to proceed entirely by compass. Shackleton, who did the navigating, foolishly took his goggles off to examine that compass— and was rewarded with a spell of snow blindness. He recovered; he had to.

On the 7th the snow and wind were such that the men camped for two days. They had two tents, two to a tent, each with a separate sleeping bag. Shackleton decreed that they should switch tent companions every week, for he feared that there might otherwise develop "sides". This was probably true. Adams and Marshall had been close friends from the beginning, and had shared a cubicle at base, whereas little Frank Wild was almost embarrassingly devoted to the Boss.

November 14th, as they were camping for the night, they found themselves within sight of Depot A, where, the next day, they rested a bit, deposited some supplies, and repacked.

November 16th was a good day. They made 17 miles, reaching the 80th parallel of latitude.

The snow had grown crusty, and the ponies were having a heavy time of it, for they would sink in sometimes clear up to their bellies. Chinaman in particular obviously was suffering and could no longer pull his weight, so on November 21st they shot him and cut up his body. They got 50 pounds of meat out of Chinaman. If they were a mite queasy about eating this, just at first, they kept their queasiness to themselves, for they had known for a long time that horse probably would be part of their diet before they got back. To their pleased surprise Chinaman tasted like beef—tough beef, true, but beef all the same.

November 22nd the weather cleared, and they reached Depot B. Here Adams had trouble with a tooth, and Dr. Marshall, after several tries, pulled it.

November 26th they passed, by two miles, Scott's farthest-south, and reached Depot C, where they left still more supplies they hoped to pick up on the way back. Here Grisi was shot and cut up. They had done more than 300 miles in a month, and were proud of themselves.

Quan quit and was killed December 1st. This left only Socks, which would whimper at night, for it missed its companions, but which in the daytime continued to pull as best it could. Each of the men had "adopted" one of the ponies back at base, making friends with it. Socks was Wild's and he tried to comfort it in its lonesomeness.

December 2nd they started up a glacier they couldn't avoid, the one Shackleton had named after his patron, Sir William Beardmore. The going was arduous. Often they had to relay, and sometimes they had to cut footholds in the ice. When they made three miles in a day—and they pulled for nine hours at a stretch—they considered that very good. They established Depot D on the glacier. It had been a part of Shackleton's plan to set up a depot every 100 miles, marking each with flags, and, of course, each lightened the load a little.

Every man kept a diary—almost every man on the entire expedition kept a diary—for they were conscious of their historic importance. This is what Frank Wild wrote in his diary the night of December 7th:

"I was very nearly finished diary writing today. We started at 8 A.M. this morning keeping rather close to the W. side of glacier, as the pressure ridges were not far away. The surface was dreadfully soft, we were sinking knee deep, and poor Socks was often in to his belly. Shortly after getting under way we got amongst crevasses again and made out towards the centre of the glacier. Several times Socks got his feet through the bridges (all the crevasses here are snow bridged and difficult to see) and twice got his hind quarters in. S.A. and M. often walked over them without breaking them at all, but Socks being so much heavier, and having smaller feet went through, and I felt rather uneasy, as leading him I should stand a very good chance of going with him, especially as he required holding back all the time.

"We camped at 1 P.M. for lunch, with a crevasse about 5 yards away on either side of us. After lunch, making for the centre of the glacier we got a much better surface, and the sledges were running nicely; S.A. and M. were 10 yards ahead, when I suddenly stepped into space, felt a violent blow on my shoulder and a fearful rush of something past me, a vicious snatch at my right hand, and found myself hanging by my left arm only, in a horrible chasm, Socks gone, and the sledge with a broken bow very nearly following; I got out somehow, and the other three running back, we quickly got the sledge into safety. Socks must have been killed instantly, as we could hear no sound from below, and see nothing but an intense black depth."

Socks had been helping only spottily, at this stage, but it *had* been helping, right up to the end. Now each man had to haul 250 pounds, and there was more relaying than ever. They began to weaken, though they would not admit it.

They had cut down on their daily food ration, Spartan though this was. Customarily they would have for breakfast a small hoosh (nobody knows where this word came from: some Eskimo dialect, perhaps?) or thick heavy soup, together with one biscuit; for lunch some lump chocolate, a cup of tea, and four biscuits; and for dinner a whole pot of hoosh, a pannikin of cocoa, and three biscuits. Of the pony meat they still had left they used some in the hooshes and the rest they stashed at the various depots.

December 15th there was a slight change in the conditions of travel. The men were still climbing, but there was a better surface and they no longer needed to relay, which was a vast relief.

December 17th they established Depot E.

December 20th they were able to take a sun sight, the first one in a long while, and they worked it out that they were at latitude 85 degrees 17 minutes. They were 8,000 feet above sea level, but the ground ahead of them still rose.

Christmas Eve they got out of the crevasse country and discarded one sledge.

Christmas Day they treated themselves to a feast. Besides the regular rations, Frank Wild cracked out a plum pudding, and they ate this cooked in cocoa, after which they sipped a little of the brandy from the medicine chest. Dr. Marshall took their temperatures, and each was two degrees below normal, which was not alarming in the circumstances. Otherwise they were in excellent shape.

On December 30th a blizzard blew up that kept them confined to their tents for a couple of days. The air was not notably cold, only about 20 below, but the wind was terrible, the snow blinding. They were all very hungry, and they kept thinking about food, and writing about it in their diaries, and, whenever they had a chance, talking about it among themselves, just as Scott, Shackleton, and Billy Wilson had done six years ago.

New Year's Day of 1909 they found themselves at 87 degrees six and a half minutes south latitude, which beat even the northern record, the Arctic record. They were nearer to the South Pole, that is, than Captain Peary had ever been to the North Pole. But they knew that they couldn't go much farther. They had talked it over. They could make it to the Pole, they agreed, but if they did they would never return.

January 4th they optimistically established yet another depot, F. And they trudged achingly on. The going was easier now. The ground had leveled off. They were on a plateau.

January 7th they had just about decided to turn back when a blizzard hit them. For two days they had to stay in their tents.

On a glorious, clear, sunny morning, January 9th, they came out running. Literally. They left behind them their rations and equipment, their tents and sledges, their medicine, their maps, their precious diaries, their rock samples, and carried only a camera, a sextant, a brass capsule containing New Zealand stamps, and the Union Jack that the King had given them.

Side by side they ran, arms outspread. They went straight south for as far as they could hold out. They stopped, a little over 97 miles from the South Pole.

They took a sight. They planted the Union Jack. They buried the stamps. They solemnly proclaimed the whole plateau to be a part of the British Empire; and then they lined up, Adams, Wild, Marshall, next to the flag, while Shackleton took their picture.

After that there was nothing for them to do but go home. If they could get there. Had a blizzard struck then, obliterating their footprints, they would be doomed to death. They had taken that chance when they started to run.

Here's what Shackleton wrote in his diary that night:

"The last day out we have shot our bolt and the tale is 88.23 S. 162 E. The wind eased down at 1 A.M. At 2 A.M. we were up, had breakfast and shortly after 4 A.M. started south with the Union Jack and the brass Cylinder of Stamps. At 9 A.M. hard quick marching we were in 88.23 and there hoisted H.M.'s flag, took possession of the Plateau in the name of H.M. and called it *K.E.* Plat. Rushed back over a surface, hardened somewhat by the recent wind and had lunch, took photo of camp Furthest South and then got away marching till 5 P.M. dead tired. Camped lovely night—19 [19 below zero]. Homeward Bound. Whatever regrets may be, we have done our best. Beaten the South Record by 366 miles the North by 77 miles. Amen."

They had a fete that night with a sip of—of all things—sloe gin; and Wild smoked a cigar he had saved, his last.

The return was a nightmare. Going down the Beardmore Glacier was faster than going up it had been, but at the same time more dangerous, and rougher, for they had to hurry lest they starve. Adams collapsed, but was revived and staggered on. Wild, even tough little Frankie Wild, collapsed; but he too was revived, and he too carried on.

They took all sorts of chances leaping crevasses rather than looking for a way to get around them, for hours, maybe even minutes, were precious now.

Shackleton had a racking headache much of the time, probably because of his empty stomach. What hurt him even worse was the fear that he might be letting his men down.

"The worst of it with him he worries so much because he thinks he is delaying us," Wild wrote in his diary the night of January 23rd, "but on this horrible ice we could not possibly go any faster, or we should break up both ourselves and sledge in very short time."

They had only one sledge left then.

They raised every depot of food, though not often with much time to spare. Once they had to go 40 hours without solid food, and mighty little liquid. Their heels and toes, their shins and knees, their hands as well, were chipped and cracked and cut from falling, for they could scarcely stand. Each was a mass of bruises.

Some of the cached horse meat seemed to have gone bad—or perhaps it had been bad in the first place. At any rate, all day February 4th they lay in their tents, so sick with dysentery that they could not stir. The next morning it was touch and go and they almost thought to quit, to die there, give up. But they rose, somehow. They carried on.

February 15th was Shackleton's 35th birthday, but they had no spirit for celebration.

February 20th they picked up Depot A, though they almost missed it because of the phenomenon called "ice blink."

That left only one more depot, the one planted the previous autumn at Minna's Bluff by the supporting party, which no doubt had visited it since. They learned, when they got there February 23rd, that this was so. The place had been restocked, and there was news for them: the *Nimrod* was back, on schedule. But when would she sail?

Now they had porridge, that goo so dear to the hearts of Englishmen. They had sausage. They had eggs, and even jam. Inevitably, though they tried not to, they overate. Dr. Marshall, the very one who should have known better, showed the greatest reaction. His dysentery returned with a vengeance, and next morning he had trouble getting to his feet. The morning after that he was forbidden to even try. Adams was left to care for him in a tent and Wild and the Boss started a last sprint for the *Discovery* hut and relief.

They reached the hut the night of February 26th, and by means of an oil lamp signaled to the *Nimrod* out in McMurdo Sound. Their signals were seen by a man who had been posted with a glass in the crow's nest for that very purpose, and the two were rescued the next morning—in the automobile.

Ernest Shackleton allowed himself three hours of sleep, and then he rose to lead a relief party in person. They rescued Adams and Dr. Marshall. They caught the *Nimrod* in time. They started home.

These men were failures. They had not discovered the South Pole. But they had travelled 1,613 miles over the most difficult terrain in the world, and more than half of that was ground upon which the foot of man had never before been placed, and they had lived for 126 days on rations calculated to last 91 days—with care. They had nothing to be ashamed of.

CHAPTER 10

THE WORLD was dash-mad. From north as from south, often at the same time, confusingly but excitingly came tales of derring-do and desperate endurance on ice, together with a spate of old words used in a new way, a distinctively polar way, and fascinating new words—blubber, brash, williwaws, sennegrass, hoosh, finnskoes, pemmican, sastrugi, huskies, ninataks, igloo, penguin, and many more.

The technique was familiar, yet it always seemed fresh. A doughty explorer, having spent years in preparation, put everything into one last plunge, whether south or north, by a superhuman effort getting as near as he could get to a pole, and then went home to write a book. These books sold very well.

In England, Shackleton had just returned from the bottom of the world, a place to which Scott was preparing to go, and popular rumor held these men to be rivals. Amundsen the Norwegian, Arctowski the Belgian, and dapper, elegant little Dr. Charcot in France, all were organizing polar parties. All this was titillating.

It remained for the United States of America, however, to give the public a real contest, a slambang fight with no holds barred, the prize a pole.

Robert Edwin Peary (pronounced *peery*) was a commander in the U.S. Navy—the regular navy, not the reserves—but he seldom did any routine duty, being carried away by his efforts to attain the top of the world. For 23 years he had been so striving, and he was 52 when at last, April 6th, 1909, on his eighth try, he reached his goal. He was in the company of four Eskimos and his personal servant Matthew Henson, a Negro. He took sundry soundings and observations, erected a pole, and ran up the Stars and Stripes, and after 30 hours started south for Greenland. When he arrived at Indian Harbor, an outpost of civilization, September 6th, it was to learn that only a few days earlier another American explorer, Dr. Frederick A. Cook, had wired triumphantly to the *New York Herald* from the Shetland Islands that *he* had reached the North Pole April 21st of the *previous* year, 1908. Cook had been missing for a long time, and assumed dead. Peary knew Cook, and didn't like him. Cook was an amiable, affable, eager man who got along well in any company, and Peary, who had dark red hair, sweeping mustachios, and blue-gray, no-nonsense eyes, was by instinct wary of personable persons. So he sat down and wrote a telegram to the United Press: "Cook's story should not be taken seriously. Two Eskimos who accompanied him say he went no distance north and not out of sight of land. Other tribesmen corroborate."

Peary's own journalistic sponsor was *The New York Times,* and he wrote a telegram for that paper, advising it to discount the Cook story. "He has simply handed the public a gold brick," he said in part. Then he got worried, and he called in an aide, Donald MacMillan.

"What's a synonym for gold brick?"

"I don't know any. As far as I know there's no word just like it in the English language."

"It's an ugly word," said the commander. "I don't like to use it. Let's think it over for a little while."

They did this, but they got nowhere, so Peary sent the telegram. It was to hurt him a lot more than it hurt Dr. Cook.

In Copenhagen, the first city he visited, Cook was given a tumultuous greeting by serious scientists. He told them that he had been accompanied to the pole by two Eskimos, Etukishook and Ahwelah, taking a route roughly parallel to that to be taken a year later by Peary, though a little farther to the west. He claimed to have sighted a new land far north of Greenland, though he did not visit it, being absorbed by his dash. He got hopelessly lost on the way back, he said, and it took him a long time—assumed to be a whole year—to find his base again. He was vague about how he had lived and what he had done during that year.

Cook was a shy, pleasant-spoken man, with a manner that was almost childlike, and the Danes doused him with adulation. It was not so in England and America, where scientists and explorers were more skeptical. Meanwhile, too, the approaching Peary had spoken by wire in no uncertain tones; and even those who did not like Peary—and they were many—respected him. If the commander was not one to pull punches, neither was he a man to put on an act just for the sake of acting. "The more dramatic your expeditions are, the more incompetent you are," he used to say; and he should know, having led so many.

"Maybe there are two North Poles," the wags said.

"The question used to be, what lies about the North Pole," the *New York World* remarked. "Now it is *who* lies about it?"

Just at first, in America at least, the general public was inclined to give Dr. Cook the benefit of the doubt. This was not because of any proof that the man produced—for his "proof" was airy at best—but rather because of his diffident smile in contrast with the bluster of Commander Peary. That "gold brick" telegram had made a big impact. To call a man a liar from a distance, before you had even pretended to examine his proofs, if any, or given him a chance to defend himself, simply was not sporting. Peary, to be sure, had no interest in being sporting. He went into the fight hammer and tongs, his customary style.

"It will be best to have the *South* Pole discovered by one man at a time," commented the *Indianapolis Star*.

Each explorer was made much of by scientific societies and lecture audiences.

72

Peary said that he had caused the Eskimos, Ahwelah and Etukishook, to be carefully questioned, and that they had denied that they had made a dash for the Pole with Cook. They'd never left Greenland, they said. Cook said that he had instructed them not to tell anybody about the dash because he wished to break the news to a waiting world himself when he got out. The public *hmmmed*.

Cook was liked everywhere for his ingratiating ways. Peary only added to the number of his enemies. There were those who thought that he played too rough with poor little Dr. Cook. Many high-ranking Navy officers disliked him because while they were doing the dreary routine in Washington and at sea, maintaining their service, he was racing back and forth across the frozen north—much of the time, thanks to a friend in the White House called Roosevelt, on full pay. All the same, and in spite of some spirited opposition, Peary was raised to a captaincy and soon afterward was retired with the rank of rear admiral. He never made another Arctic trip, but took up flying instead—at 53.

There were some, especially in the South, who frowned upon Peary because he had taken a Negro instead of a white man to the Pole with him. The governor of Georgia and the mayor of Atlanta refused to greet Peary when he went there to give a lecture.

"Henson was the best man for the job," protested MacMillan. Peary himself probably never gave the matter a thought. Henson had gone on each of the previous expeditions and undoubtedly knew the business, as evidenced by the fact that he too, on his return, wrote a book.

"England is raising $200,000 to send Captain Scott to the South Pole," commented the *Washington Times*. "About $183,000 of that had better be used to get a good umpire."

There was no open scandal, nobody was officially disgraced, and the cause of polar exploration, which depends so much on well-wishers, *rich* well-wishers, was not crippled. Cook, whose claim to have been the first man to scale Mount McKinley was also held in serious doubt, had his believers to the bitter end; but they became fewer all the time; and when at last a special committee at the University of Copenhagen, the scene of his first resounding triumph, examined his proofs and pronounced them insufficient to establish his claim, the controversy was generally considered dead.

Peter Freuchen, the explorer, who knew both men, summed it up: "Cook was a liar and a gentleman. Peary was neither."

CHAPTER 11

JUST BEING a hero is not in itself full-time, paying employment. Ernest Henry Shackleton was famous, but he was still far from the fortune he craved. Indeed, the problem that faced him immediately, if not publicly, was the need to raise more money. The expedition was over, but it hadn't been paid for. The figures were all in his head or in his own private books; he was the most unbusinesslike of men, and answerable to no man or organization, but it is certain that they were big figures, smashers. Naively he had once estimated that the expedition to Antarctica would cost about £17,000, complete. In fact, it was costing almost three times that. Nor was the end of expenditure in sight. The men had to be got home and paid off. The scientists had to be supported while they were assembling and recording and evaluating their findings, a job that might take a year. The *Nimrod,* whether she was to be used again or simply sold, needed a thorough overhaul. Biggest of all loomed the debts. He hoped that he could persuade at least a few of the creditors to change their loans to outright gifts, and he would set about this effort immediately.

He was amazed, though not displeased, to find that he was a hero. After all, he had failed. He hadn't brought the South Pole home, to lay at Emily's feet. Yet his own personality, no less than the drama of the dash, had caught the public's imagination, and he was huzzaed wherever he went. It was his duty to cash in on this for all it was worth. He was honor-bound to make money.

At first, in New Zealand, and a little later in Australia, on the way home, he pursued his previous policy of turning over his lecture fees to charity; but he realized that once he got back to England he should go about it in a cold commercial way, putting himself into the hands of an agency. It is notable that when he left New Zealand he had in company a young newspaperman, Edward Saunders, who was already working with him on the production of the inevitable book.

His reception at home was tumultuous. The public took him to its heart. He was handsome, clear-cut, with fine blue-gray eyes, a boy's-book hero with a square jaw, a bluff manner, a sense of humor, and, unexpectedly, no airs. He might have been called, and perhaps he was, England's answer to Richard Harding Davis. Everywhere he went, crowds cheered, and his lecture agent assured him that he would have capacity halls for years to come at home and abroad, "abroad" included the States where the public was eager to see him again.

The King received him and made him a commander of the Royal Victorian Order. The King at the same time gave him and each of his fellow members of the expedition the Polar Cross, bronze for those who had manned the *Nimrod,* silver for those of the land party. The Royal Geographical Society gave him a sumptuous dinner at which he was awarded the Society's gold medal. On December 14th he was knighted.

The accolade, which astonished no one, at least made things easier for the newspaper reporters, who, insistent that every man must have some sort of title, had been calling the lion Lieutenant Shackleton, a practice that brought about a spate of testy letters from Royal Navy officers, pointing out that the returned explorer was no longer even a *reserve* lieutenant. Hereafter he was to be Sir Ernest. And Emily was Lady Shackleton.

The reporters never would let him and Robert Falcon Scott alone, but pestered them with questions about their plans as they moved from place to place, raising funds, holding conferences. Were they involved in a race? Was this to be a dash to the death? Would one break his neck to get there before the other?

Shackleton—he was sometimes called, behind his back, Ernest Almost Shackleton—remained circumspect, determinedly uncommunicative. Scott's plans were well formed, and there was no doubt that he would get away first. Shackleton's plans, though he refused to say so, depended upon what Scott did or failed to do.

Neither could be teased or taunted into making an impetuous answer, and when they met in public, they were proper. They may not have been warm, but they were correct.

Each had his adherents in the Royal Geographic Society and no doubt in the general public as well; attempts were made to have them declare an open feud but they were much too well guarded for this. Not only were their manners in public impeccable—Shackleton even made a few speeches to help Scott collect money—but their correspondence was carried on with a formality so stiff as to suggest the correspondence that precedes a duello. Thus, in July of 1909:

"Dear Shackleton:

"If, as I understand, it does not cut across any future plan of yours, I propose to organize the Expedition to the Ross Sea which, as you know, I have had so long in preparation so as to start next year.

"My plan is to establish a base in King Edward Land and to push South and East. I cannot but think that late in the season with a heavier ship than the *Nimrod* it will be possible to establish the base.

"The prospect offers good geographical work as well as a chance of reaching a high latitude, and I am sure you will wish me success; but of course I should be glad to have your assurance that I am not disconcerting any plan of your own."

To which Shackleton replied:

"Dear Captain Scott:

"I understand that you have already your expedition in preparation, and it will not interfere with any plans of mine. If I do any further exploration it will not be until I have news of your expedition, presuming that you start next year. I may later on attempt the circumnavigation of the Antarctic Continent but my ideas as regards this are indefinite.

"I wish you every success in your endeavour to penetrate the ice and to land on King Edward VII Land and to attain a high latitude from that base. I quite agree with you that good geographical work can be done from that quarter, and it will have a newer interest than McMurdo Sound."

Shackleton, hating it but doing it extremely well, went on lecturing, in England, Scotland, Canada, the United States, Germany, France, Scandanavia. He even visited St. Petersburg and was received by the Czar. He was heaped with honors. He fooled around with some dark Hungarian mining concessions that were supposed to make millions but somehow didn't; but he could not really do anything definite until he saw what happened to the man whose turn it now was— Robert Falcon Scott.

His book, *The Heart of the Antarctic,* punctuation by Saunders, was published in two volumes, appearing simultaneously in seven languages, November 14th, 1909. It did well, but was no answer to the problem.

The *Nimrod,* complete with a spread of Antarctic exhibits—miniature dog sleds and the like—was thrown open to the public in London and in many other English cities. This brought in more than £3,000, a drop in the bucket. Shackleton's financial plight was not even cleared up when the government, in response to a public clamor, picked up the tab to the tune of £20,000, though assuredly that helped.

Scott sailed south June 15th, 1911 to a fate that was to shock the world.

CHAPTER 12

ROALD ENGEBREGHT GRAVNING AMUND-
SEN was a dour, long-faced, sardonic man, a ro-
manticist at heart perhaps, but the face he
showed to the world was hard, harsh, and impla-
cable. His mother had wanted him to be a doctor,
and to please her he had studied medicine for two
years. But what he really aspired to be was an
Arctic explorer. He wanted to discover the North
Pole. He had been to the Antarctic too, but that
did not interest him.

He managed to raise enough money to buy
Nansen's *Fram*, a wooden vessel built especially
for polar work, and he enlisted a crew of 18,
besides himself, all carefully hand-picked, all in
perfect condition. He bought 116 dogs, which
were to be allowed the run of the deck.

He was all set to sail when word came that the
North Pole *had* just been discovered, by Peary.
Disgusted, but not disheartened, Amundsen decided then to go to the the South Pole instead. His
men were willing. His equipment would be as
good there as in the north. He started out.

Now he knew that the Englishman, Captain

Scott, already was on his way to Antarctica, but, after all, the English did not have any legal monopoly on that continent, though they sometimes acted as if they thought they did. Amundsen did, however, on his way south, send to Scott from Madeira a message formally advising him of his intentions. Scott was at Sydney, and this message made him feel bad.

Scott had been feeling pretty bad anyway. He had been moody, irritable. Perhaps he sensed what was coming.

The weather between New Zealand and Antarctica gave him plenty of cause for complaint. Overloaded, the little *Terra Nova* was caught in a storm that tossed her on her beam-ends time after time, so that the wonder was she didn't broach to and capsize. The pumps broke down. The cargo shifted. Of the 19 ponies and 33 dogs they carried on deck, two ponies and one dog were lost. But they finally made it.

As Shackleton had done a few years earlier, Scott tried to land on Edward VII Land, and as Shackleton had done, he learned that he could not; so he made once again for McMurdo Sound. Even there he had to wait for almost a month before the ice would permit him to land his supplies. He did not use either his own old *Discovery* hut or the hut Shackleton's party had left, though both were in good condition. He put up another hut about halfway between these two.

Then he thought of the Bay of Whales, a good anchorage in the Ross Ice Shelf. It was farther east, but it was also farther south. It would be about 60 miles nearer to the Pole than was the shore of McMurdo Sound. He sent his second-in-command, Campbell, to have a look. Campbell found the Norwegians under Amundsen already there, snug, and prepared to wait out the winter and then make a dash for it.

Everything was cordial. The Norwegians invited the English to dinner, and the English reciprocated. Conversation was easy; there was no shop talk. After a while the English departed.

They had been struck by the smooth, quiet efficiency of the camp. There had been no fuss, no clutter of scientific instruments, no elaborate records. These Norwegians were not interested in flora and fauna—if any—in temperatures, atmospheric conditions, salinity, or rock samples. They were interested in one thing only—getting to the South Pole. They made no bones about this.

The Norwegians, too, seemed to see nothing miraculous in the fact that the Bay of Whales, after a wait of only two days, was clear of ice long enough to let them in. Nobody ever before or since has seen the Bay of Whales clear of ice,

To be a successful pole discoverer you must have patience, ingenuity, fortitude, great skill, determination, physical strength, adaptability, and luck; and it is by no means certain that the last is the least important.

Scott's party was to consist of himself; Dr. E. A. Wilson, the same "Billy" who had made the previous try with Scott and with Shackleton; Lieutenant H. R. "Birdie" Bowers, R.N.; Captain L.E.G. Oates of the Inniskilling Dragoons; and a navy enlisted man named Edgar Evans, who was husky and willing, a doer. They set forth November 1st, 1911, accompanied by two supporting parties, one to take them across the ice shelf, the other to go as far as the Beardmore Glacier. The supporting parties had dogs to pull their sledges, but the dash party itself was to rely on ponies. Scott distrusted dogs. He never could be tough enough with them.

Going over the glacier was rugged, and even after they had reached the polar plateau, which Shackleton had found comparatively easily, they faced treacherous surfaces, intense cold, a wind that was all knives. The men wore skis part of the time, and part of the time finnskoes; it depended upon the nature of the surface, which was always changing. The ponies tried hard, but they were not much help, and before the party reached the South Pole, January 17th, 1912, all the ponies had either died or been shot.

For they did reach the Pole. They knew it immediately, not merely because their instruments told them but also because the place was marked with a black tent, over which floated the flag of Norway.

Amundsen had gotten there first.

While discouraging in the extreme, this was not altogether a surprise. In the previous week they had several times seen sledge and dog tracks and the remains of camps.

Amundsen had reached the Pole December 14th, 1911, a month before Scott, and with four followers. He had used only dogs, taking 52 of the

116 he had brought out, and returned with eleven of these. He had crossed the Axel Heiberg Glacier, a much less formidable one than the Beardmore, and had made the whole trip in 99 days. Even while Scott and his men were staggering into the tent he had left, he was on his way back, taking his time, with more supplies than he needed.

There were two letters in the tent. One was addressed to the King of Norway; the other, in English, was addressed to Robert Falcon Scott. Amundsen asked the English leader to deliver the letter to the King only in the event that Amundsen did not survive the trip back to civilization. This was not meant to be ironic.

Well, there was nothing to keep them there. They took a few shots of the sun and made a few soundings, and the next day they departed, pulling their remaining sledge.

They had not until that time realized how much the trip had taken out of them. They were all weak, and they often stumbled and fell. Worse, when they started to pick up their supply depots on the way back, they learned that much of the fuel oil had somehow evaporated. That meant many a cold meal.

"Must fight it out to the last biscuit," Scott wrote in his diary.

Evans was the first to go. He was the biggest, by far the strongest—the other four were small men—and it amazed them that he went so suddenly, so dramatically.

It would not have amazed Rear Admiral Robert

Edwin Peary (U.S.N., ret.), for Peary always distrusted heavy men. He insisted that anyone who went on his expeditions weigh no more than two and a half pounds for every inch of height. He himself stood an even six feet.

Evans fell down a crevasse. This was happening to them all the time on the glacier, as it had happened to Shackleton, Adams, Dr. Marshall, and Wild. Evans must have hit his head, for though Dr. Wilson could find nothing obviously wrong with him, thereafter he acted queer. He was pitifully weak, and they did not make him pull a sledge, permitting him to tag along behind. He fell back, and they waited for him to catch up. He fell back again, and this time, though they waited, he did not reappear. They went back, and found him on hands and knees, "a wild look" in his eyes. They lifted him to his feet, but he collapsed again. They made camp then and there, hoping that some hot food would revive him, but he passed into a coma and died a few hours later. They left him there.

Captain Oates, sometimes playfully called Titus, was suffering from frostbitten feet. It was horribly painful for him to walk. He never complained, but they could see it in his face. He thought he was holding them back, and he begged them to leave him in his sleeping bag to die. They refused.

There came a time in March (just a few days after Amundsen had sailed into Hobart, Tasmania, to announce his discovery of the South

Pole) when they were trapped by a blizzard. As Oates got into his sleeping bag that night, he expressed the hope that he would never get out of it again, never wake up. It seemed likely. He also expressed the hope that his regiment would approve of the way he went to his death. The Inniskillings were a proud outfit.

He did wake up in the morning, and the storm still raged. It was March 16th, a Friday. To go out in that blow more than a few feet from the tent would be simple suicide; and he knew this. He toddled to the flap.

"I'm just going outside and may be some time," he said carelessly.

They tried to talk him out of it, but he went. They never saw him again.

The other three, when the elements had subsided, staggered on a little farther, but were overtaken by another blizzard. They were only eleven miles from the next depot, but they knew that they would never make it. They pitched the tent and prepared to die.

They had talked it over, dispassionately. The instinct of each was to go on walking, without the sledge, until they dropped in their tracks. But if they did that, all their papers and records and diaries would be lost, as would the 35 pounds of rock samples Dr. Wilson had collected. They decided to stay in the tent and wait for the end to come.

Captain Scott wrote letters to the widows-to-be, and also to Sir James Barrie, the playwright, and other personal friends. He stacked the letters neatly.

Then he made one last entry in his diary:

"Thursday, March 29—Since the 21st we have had a continuous gale from W.S.W. and S.W. We had fuel to make two cups of tea apiece and bare food for two days on the 20th. Every day we have been ready to start for our depot *11 miles* away, but outside the door of the tent it remains a scene of whirling drift. I do not think we can hope for any better things now. We shall stick it out to the end, but we are getting weaker, of course, and the end cannot be far.

"It seems a pity, but I do not think I can write more.

R. Scott

"Last entry. For God's sake, look after our people."

Not for seven months, not until October 12th, did a relief party find the tent. The bodies were in a perfect state of preservation, as bodies always are in Antarctica.

CHAPTER 13

WHAT DID THIS leave for Ernest Henry Shack leton? His life was dedicated to the Antarctic continent, which held all of his hopes of fortune. Where could he turn now? What sensational trip could he make, after two parties already had reached the South Pole? What would overshadow that great feat?

He had an answer. He announced the formation of the Imperial Trans-Antarctic Expedition with offices at 4 New Burlington Street.

He would go not merely to the Pole but through it.

Antarctica, the continent, is almost perfectly round. The Antarctic Circle in effect comprises its northern boundary. At only one point does the continent extend any mentionable distance north of the Circle, and that is the peninsula, presently called the Antarctic Peninsula (see Appendix A), which reaches like a long accusatory finger pointing to the southern tip of South America, of which it might at one time have been a part. There are, however, two large dents in this perimeter, two bites, as it were, on opposite sides of the pie. One of these is just east of the Antarctic Peninsula—that is, southeast of Cape Horn, of Tierra del Fuego. It is the Weddell Sea, named for the English skipper who discovered it, and customarily jammed with dangerous ice packs, a good place to keep away from. On the other side of the continent, just south of New Zealand, is the Ross Sea, which includes McMurdo Sound, jumping-off place for both of Scott's expeditions and for Shackleton's previous independent expedition.

Shackleton proposed to send out two vessels. One from New Zealand or Australia—probably New Zealand—would sail to McMurdo Sound and establish a base there, out of which sundry scientific parties could sally. The real purpose of this base, though, was to lay a series of food and fuel depots almost to the South Pole, over territory Shackleton had already traveled. Meanwhile the Boss, Sir Ernest, would proceed from Buenos Aires in another vessel to the Weddell Sea, where he would establish a base on the mainland if possible, on the ice if necessary. From this base there would proceed two geological parties, east and west. Again, the main purpose of the base would be to get the dash party launched. The preliminary work would be done by two sledges equipped with aeroplane engines and propellers. This would save the dogs (for Shackleton was on dogs again, and off ponies), which would follow. The party of four or five—conceivably six— would carry all its own supplies, and it would not establish depots. It would go to the pole, and keep going, picking up, one by one, on the other side of the continent, the depots previously placed there by the McMurdo Sound party. This plan called for careful consideration and, for very nice timing; otherwise it would be calamitous. The distance is about 1,800 miles.

Many members of the Royal Geographical Society shook their heads. It all sounded too flamboyant to them, something designed exclusively for the glorification and enrichment of Ernest Henry Shackleton, while the scientific aspects, of which so much was made, they regarded as no more than window trimming. They were especially shocked by the proposal to take along a couple of propeller-driven sledges. It was done only for purposes of publicity, they averred.

The aeroplane engine idea, in fact, was not Shackleton's own but that of Douglas Mawson, the Australian scientist who had gone on the 1908-9 expedition. He was one of those who turned up the South Magnetic Pole, and had since made an expedition of his own to Antarctica. Mawson had experimented with a plane with clipped wings and with skis instead of landing gear. Shackleton had even hired Mawson's mechanic, an Australian, who was to have charge of the two propeller-driven sledges. These were not expected to make long trips, for they burned too much gasoline, and they would, of course, be worse than useless on the glacier, but it was hoped that they could do much of the early hauling.

The Society eventually granted Shackleton a nominal £2,000, but many of the members remained skeptical.

The government, properly prodded, put up £10,000 on condition that Shackleton could raise a similar sum from private sources. This he did, for he was getting quite good at soliciting money. Rather unexpectedly he persuaded Sir James Caird, a Scottish manufacturer of jute, who until that time had taken no interest in polar or any other kind of exploration, to contribute £24,000, without strings.

Even so, he was going to have to mortgage the enterprise, as he had done with the *Nimrod* expedition, raising promises of loans rather than immediate cash, and pre-allocating lecture fees and book royalties. All of this, of course, was predicated on the assumption that he himself, Sir Ernest Shackleton, would survive. What if he died? As before, he was running a one-man show.

No doubt the name Imperial Trans-Antarctic Expedition had been selected with care. Imperial, not just British. There was a chance that he might get some money from Australia and New Zealand, as before, and perhaps even from Canada. He had been popular in Canada when he lectured there, and at one time had even toyed with the idea of doing a little exploring in the upper MacKenzie country.

Besides, it was a good time to touch the strings of patriotism. This is not to imply that Shackleton was a hypocrite. He was sincerely a patriotic man. But he could hardly fail to note that the British people, with their long and commendable record of exploration in both the Arctic and Antarctic regions, had felt, if only instinctively, that they were entitled to bag the poles.

"From the sentimental point of view," Shackleton wrote in his prospectus, "it is the last great polar journey that can be made. It will be a greater journey than the journey to the Pole and back, and I feel that it is up to the British nation to accomplish this, for we have been beaten at the conquest of the North Pole and beaten at the first conquest of the South Pole. There now remains the largest and most striking of all journeys—the crossing of the Continent."

From Sir Douglas Mawson—he had been knighted because of his expedition-leading scientific activities in the Antarctic, subsequent to the *Nimrod* expedition—Shackleton purchased, at long distance, the *Aurora,* a vessel much like Scott's *Terra Nova,* a sealer, and stout. This was to carry the Ross Sea party. Lieutenant Aeneas Mackintosh, who had been a member of the *Nimrod* expedition, was to have charge of her and of the whole party.

From Lars Christensen, the Norwegian whaling magnate, Shackleton bought the *Polaris,* a real bargain. She had just been built, in the famous Framnaes shipyards at Sandefjord, by men who had themselves ventured into Arctic waters, and with the advice of Baron de Gerlache, a Belgian who had headed an 1897 Antarctic expedition. She was made of the finest and strongest pine, oak, and greenheart, a wood that weighed more than iron, especially stressed against ice floes. She had been designed to take parties of rich men to the Arctic on polar bear hunts, which were popular at that time, but when de Gerlache got into financial trouble and had to drop out of the partnership, Christensen let her go cheap—a mere £14,000. She must have cost much more than that to build. She was a vessel of lovely lines, a thing to boast about, barkentine-rigged—that is, carrying a square sail on the foremast, fore-and-aft sails on the other two masts, and in addition she was equipped with triple-expansion engines that could drive her up to ten knots. She was rated at 350 tons. Shackleton, delighted, changed her name to *Endurance*, from his family motto: *Fortitudine vincimus*.

The tragic deaths of Captain Scott and his companions had done nothing to intimidate the English, and when Shackleton at last publicly announced his intention of going out again, he was swamped with applications—more than 5,-000 of them, including one from "three sporty girls" who would be willing, and indeed would "just love," if they were taken, to wear pants.

He went about his recruiting in the same happy-go-lucky manner as he had done the previous time, selecting a little group of veterans at first but taking or rejecting the others apparently by hunch, after interviews that seldom lasted longer than five minutes.

Frank Wild was balding a bit, but he was as wiry as ever. He would be second in command. Thomas Crean, a bulky young Navy veteran—

most of the men, like Wild, were small—was to be second officer. He was Irish, and he knew his business. Alfred Cheetham, exceptionally small, was third officer. Thomas McLeod, who had served with Shackleton before, was one of the seamen. And "Putty" Marston the artist who, unlike most of the others, was married, brought his paints aboard, all a-grin.

There was no grinning about Harry "Chippy" McNeish, the carpenter, a burly Scot, as sharp as a crab apple and about as desirable, a tart, touchy, argumentative man, such as most skippers try to avoid—a sea lawyer, always yammering about his rights. At 56, McNeish was the oldest member of the crew.

Frank Worsley was 42, but Shackleton had liked him instantly. He was a New Zealander, and had been at sea since age 16. He'd had experience with sail, a point in his favor. Shackleton made him captain of the *Endurance,* which lay at the South-West India docks in London.

Young Leonard D. A. Hussey was a meteorologist just out of college, and he had been assigned to a job in the Sudan, of all places. He had come from the heart of Africa to ask to be taken along in the *Endurance.* This amused Shackleton, who promptly hired him.

Dr. James A. McIlroy had come from even farther away, from Malaya on the other side of the world. This too tickled the fancy of Shackleton, who signed him on without knowing anything about how good or poor a physician he might be. Nor did Shackleton learn until later that Dr. McIlroy was a keen bridge player. Shackleton himself loved bridge.

So it went, briskly and with bounce. On April 1st, 1914, the good ship *Endurance* dropped downstream.

War clouds were gathering and on the very day when King George, standing on the deck of the anchored vessel at the mouth of the Thames, presented Shackleton with a Union Jack—on that day, August 8th, 1914, Great Britain declared war against Germany.

Shackleton did not know what to do. On the one hand, he had here an expensively equipped and manned vessel, years of work, thousands of pounds sterling entrusted to him by many persons and institutions for one purpose and for one purpose only; and on the other hand he suspected all the men under him did not like the notion of running away from a war.

He called them together, and put it to them on deck. He proposed that they turn over the whole expedition, with vessel, supplies, plans, and manpower, to the Admiralty, to be used in any way that that august body might think best. Unanimously and instantly they agreed to this. There wasn't a whisper of dissent. Shackleton wired the offer, then waited.

He got a prompt answer, consisting of one word: "Proceed."

A few hours later, however, a more detailed telegram came. It explained that the government thought there was so much public money tied up

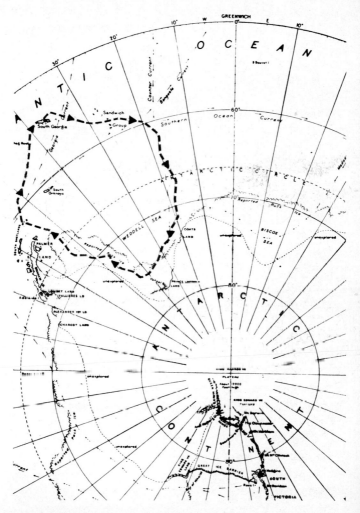

Tracing Shackleton's incredible voyage, from
the audacious start to the heroic end.

**Some members of the crew (from l. to r.):
Macauley, How, Barr, Irving and McLeod**

Dog packs are harnessed on an ice floe for safekeeping,
as the *Endurance* gradually begins to disappear into the sea.

Dome-shaped tents that could be converted into igloos were part of the equipment used by Shackleton expedition.

Trying to dig sheltering cave on Elephant Island, to be used until help arrives.

This rude wooden hut, still standing intact on Ross Island, was used as a base by the Shackleton expedition.

Boat that would provide escape once they reached open water, is dragged across ice-covered sea.

Travelling across the ice during the day, camp was pitched on a different ice floe each night.

Statue of Shackleton by Sargeant Lagger which stands
by the east wall of the Royal Geographical Society.

in this enterprise that it would be against the public interest, at this stage, to call it off. The telegram was signed by the First Lord of the Admiralty himself, a baby-faced young man named Churchill.

They went.

CHAPTER 14

THE COOK got drunk, and they fired him; he had not been a good cook anyway. This was in Buenos Aires; and to the amazement of everyone, when the word got out along the waterfront, there were 20 applicants for the job.

Surely it was not the money that attracted them. On this trip, Shackleton was paying about £50 a year for a common seaman, only about £150 for a scientist, which was low in anybody's language.

Parenthetically, the *Endurance* was insured for £10,000, of which £9,000 had been taken by Lloyd's, the rest by the Indemnity Marine Assurance Co., Ltd., of London. The premium was £665. Coverage was to be for the entire voyage and not just until the last civilized port, as had been the case with all previous arctic and antarctic expeditions.

Out of the 20 would-be cooks, some inspired person chose a small Englishman with a high squeaky voice, Charles J. Green, who proved to be a wizard—a real find.

Shackleton and Wild had not sailed with the

Endurance out of Margate, but had remained behind to settle some last-minute matters, making the trip a little later on a faster ship. Worsley was the captain during that two-month crossing, and he was too good-natured a man to be tough, with the result that discipline, at the time when Shackleton took over again, had become somewhat lax. The cook was not the only one who overcelebrated a shore leave. Two of the hands did the same and raised hell when they got back to the *Endurance,* so that they too were fired.

Still, the ship was getting crowded. Frank Hurley, an Australian who had been Mawson's official photographer and had been hired by Shackleton sight unseen, arrived to take his place. And there were 69 sled dogs from Canada housed on deck.

More than dogs came from Canada. A couple of Canadian seamen showed up, explaining that they had seen the *Endurance,* which did attract attention in Buenos Aires, and had fallen in love with her. Could they sign on?

One, William Bakewell, was 26 and an experienced mariner. They took him. The other, Percy Blackboro, was only 18, and though a strapping lad he had had very little experience at sea. They turned him down. Now there were, or should be, 27 men aboard, about equally divided among officers, seamen, and scientists.

They sailed from Buenos Aires on October 26th. Shackleton was in his cubbyhole of a cabin, worrying about money, zigzagging figures on paper. He had just arranged to send the bills for a large supply of coal and food to his agent in London, but heaven knew how that overworked man ever was going to pay them.

The *Endurance* was cheered as she cleared, and indeed she must have been a heart-lifting sight—at a distance. Up close, it was different.

The sails were furled, for the wind was not right. Everywhere on deck were piles of coal, more coal than they could possibly store below, where the bunkers were crammed. When they encountered floating ice, as they were sure to do, they must be prepared to do a great deal of backing and filling, sudden stopping, and quick changing of direction, lest they be encased in the stuff, a captive. This was the reason for the coal, which admittedly was not neat.

High in the rigging swung a ton of fresh whale meat, one little item of provisions that had not yet been paid for. It was meant for the dogs, and the dogs understandably wanted it right now. The motion of the barkentine, once it was outside, caused the meat to swing back and forth, splattering blood on the deck below. The smell of that blood was driving the dogs mad, and they yowled. Southward ho!

Everybody was in high spirits. "I wondered how our little party, now playing mouth organs, banjos and mandolins, would work and fare in the long dark days to come; the fight will be good," Shackleton wrote in his diary that first night out.

The third day, one of the seamen came to Captain Worsley on the bridge, and said, "If you would come to the locker room where the oilskins are kept, sir, I wonder whether you'd see what I think I see." Worsley went with him, and saw the same thing—a pair of feet, the lower part of a pair of legs. He hauled the fellow forth. It was young Blackboro, the Canadian kid who had wanted so badly to go to Antarctica that he persuaded some of the other seamen to hide him away.

He was brought before Sir Ernest, whose blue-gray eyes could become exceedingly steely on occasion. Sir Ernest glowered at him. He raged at him, not always as a good member of the Church of England should. He waggled a forefinger at him.

"And what's more," he finished, "if anybody has to be eaten, you'll be the first. Do you understand that?"

The poor stowaway could only nod. It was some time before he realized that he was being ribbed. He signed on as an assistant to the cook, and turned out to be very useful.

Shackleton's notion that everybody should share the work still applied here, and the scientists helped with the dishes and took their turns at the wheel the same as the others, while the forecastle hands helped to clean up the various laboratories. However, because of space, and because of the layout below decks, there was one mess hall for the hands and another for the scientists and officers. Exactly the same food in the same portions was served in each.

Though he had never been there, Shackleton knew a great deal about the Weddell Sea, for he believed in making every possible preparation. That sea is a huge, roughly circular body of water filled during most of the year, and sometimes for the entire year, with icebergs and broken, jagged floes, resembling, in Shackleton's own happy phrase, "a gigantic and interminable jigsaw puzzle". The winds there, as winds in that part of the world go, are comparatively light, which permits the formation of additional ice even in the middle of summer. These winds above, and the prevailing currents below, cause this enormous ice mass to move in a generally clockwise direction with terrible force, piling the floes against the mainland to the south, the great Antarctic Peninsula to the west. Chunks of ice that might weigh thousands of tons apiece are heaped house-high on one another.

What he had not known, and what he was to learn when they reached Grytviken, a whaling station in wild South Georgia, the farthest-south spot of civilization, was that never in the memory of the oldest skipper had the Weddell Sea ice been so thick and so far north as it was this summer. He was strongly urged not to venture down there. This advice he ignored.

Something else he learned at Grytviken was that, though the island was a British possession, the whaling business there was carried on by Argentinians and Norwegians. And very profitable it was, too. A man with a little capital to start with, say £50,000, could clean up in a place like that. Why shouldn't some Englishman get in on that business? Shackleton made a note of it. He would look further into it when he got back.

They took on more coal and whale meat at Grytviken, where they were made much of by the lonesome settlers. They lingered, for the regular supply ship from Europe was expected almost any day, and they were eager to learn how the war was coming on. It would be four months old now. Perhaps it was all over?

Another reason they wanted that supply ship was because of mail. They had given this address to the folks at home and they had all written their own last-for-a-long-while letters.

It was December 5th when they agreed that they could wait no longer, and they sailed away. Two hours later the supply ship arrived.

Two days after that, after passing between a couple of bleak and barren islands of the South Sandwich group, they came upon their first ice. It was far north of where it had any business to be, far north of the Antarctic Circle. That was ominous.

But there it was. There was the enemy.

CHAPTER 15

EVEN THE old-timers, Wild, Marston, Hurley, and Shackleton himself, those who had been out before, never ceased to marvel at the sight of the ice. Seeing it for the first time, most of the company were dazzled; they were fascinated.

It was by no means a bleak, flat-white surface. When the sun shone, it flared with every color of the rainbow, flickering brilliantly, while it floated at a majestic pace through water that was a dark turquoise-blue.

Neither was it silent, as they might have expected it to be. The floes clicked and clacked together, and groaned as they exerted resistance to shoves and bumps. When a berg calved, there was at first a high screaming noise, then a series of shotlike sounds that might have been caused by a Gatling gun, and finally a stupendous splash, a wave, a great, widespread, iridescent pittering-back. The floes bobbed to the swell of the seas, but the floating white mountains stood up to them, so that their sides were buffeted like rocky seashores, the combers banging in, thudding angrily through unseen passageways, and, hurled high into the air, settling back softly like some huge polychromatic bridal veil. Killer whales humped up underneath floes on which seals sunned themselves, and spilled these, snapping up the seals before they could swim away. Birds squawked and screeched overhead, making a querulous clamor.

Watching an iceberg, the men learned, was like watching a fire in a fireplace. It never stayed the same. It was a continuous splendor.

Now they had on their hands a fight against time. The Antarctic summer is very short, and if Shackleton did not get to a far-southerly spot where he could anchor and make his base by the end of December, he would be obliged to spend the long winter there, postponing the dash until the following spring—October, say. This did not faze him. He knew that the ice pack was unpredictable.

From the reports of two previous Weddell Sea explorers, Bruce and Filchner, he knew of the existence of a good anchorage called Vahsel Bay at the extreme southern tip of the sea—the point, that is, nearest to the Pole. This was to be his object. Meanwhile, he had somehow to get through or around the stubborn, incalculably strong, multicolored ice mass.

The first floes encountered were trifling and easily by-passed. After that, the stuff became bigger and more formidable, and they spent days and weeks looking for open sea beyond it, something to butt their way to, or suddenly opening and as suddenly shutting leads or alleys of open water, down which they might venture in a generally southern direction.

December 9th they got caught between two large hummocky floes, and the vessel was canted at a six-degree angle. They threw out an ice anchor, and the men "walked" the *Endurance* out of that tight spot by means of a capstan. A few minutes later one of the floes—really small bergs—collapsed with a prodigious roar. There but for the grace of God might have been the *Endurance*.

All of this maneuvering called for a great deal of coal, and already Shackleton was worried about his supply, though he was careful not to let this concern show. By this time, too, it had become evident that they were not going to make the big dash at least until the following summer.

It was now deep December, and light for virtually 24 hours. Even when the sun did go down for a short time around midnight, it left a glowing, pulsing twilight, so that it was never entirely dark.

In pursuance of Shackleton's policy of seizing every excuse to proclaim a celebration, they made much of Christmas—jugged hare, plum puddings, sweets, stout.

There was nothing startling in the fact that Shackleton could order Thomas Orde-Lees, the officer of Marines who was acting as a combination aeroplane engine expert and the ship's storekeeper, to crack out such a spread for this or any other occasion. He had never forgotten his own touch of scurvy and he was as fussy as a hen with only one chick about food for the members of his crew. He insisted that more than just fresh food was needed whenever obtainable, and more too than just good food. A variety of food was needed. Men can do just about anything, he used to say, if they've been properly fed. In conference with the Director of Hygiene to the War Office, Major General Wilfred Beveridge, he had devised a one-pound composition cake containing 4,000 calories, which would be a day's ration for a man working as hard as Shackleton's men would have to work. This cake, consisting of beef powder, casein, oatmeal, sugar, and oleo, to be taken cold or in a hoosh, was only for the most rugged field work. The luxuries were his own idea. He must have been the first man who ever even thought of taking jugged hare to a polar region.

The feast was followed by a songfest, for the men were in excellent spirits. Yet the sad fact remained that they were still north of the Antarctic Circle. They did not cross that line until December 30th. It was very warm, above zero.

December 31st they again got clamped between two small bergs and again had recourse to an ice anchor, the capstan, and lots of muscle to get her out before she was crushed. The *Endurance* was very strong, but a mountain of ice on either side could have flattened her.

Early in the new year of 1915 the pack cleared a bit, and they found more leads to follow.

January 5th they moored alongside a huge floe, an enormous raft of ice, and the men drew up teams and played some soccer. The day after that they exercised the dogs.

107

Three days after that, January 8th, they suddenly came upon open water. For more than a hundred miles they ran at almost full speed, south by east, and they didn't have to dodge once in that time.

Late in the afternoon of January 10th, they sighted land—Coats Land, according to their reckoning. They were only about 400 miles from Vahsel Bay.

A stretch of land that Shackleton believed had never before been seen by man he named the Caird Coast, after his benefactor, the jute magnate of Dundee.

Here they coasted at a respectful distance from the walls of ice that towered all around them, some 1,000 feet high. It was a formation similar to the Ross Ice Shelf on the opposite side of the continent, but not so big. This was the Filchner Ice Barrier. It began to look as though they might get somewhere at last.

On January 15th they saw a deep, wide bay in the glacier, a bay that was comparatively clear of ice. It had not previously been reported, and Shackleton, with no remarkable show of originality, dubbed it Glacier Bay. He was tempted to stop there and establish his camp and set up his portable hut. It would make a good anchorage, and the shore party, though it was too late to start the dash, could exercise and train the dogs, rearrange the stores, do routine scientific work, and otherwise get set for the beginning of the following spring. On the other hand, they were only about 100 miles from Vahsel Bay, and the coast looked clear. That 100 miles was practically all due south, just that much territory that the dash party would not have to cover if they camped at Vahsel Bay. He decided to go on.

It was an unfortunate decision, and one that he was soon to regret. But nobody, not even Ernest Henry Shackleton himself, ever had pretended that he was perfect.

At least, he wasted no time. He was not a man to shilly-shally.

The ice reappeared, slushy, puddinglike stuff, old and rotten, much of it caught behind a barrier made up of two huge bergs. The temperature fell sharply, and an east-northcast wind sprang up that in very short order reached gale velocity. They were at about the 76th degree of latitude.

They tried to poke a way between the bergs to what looked like open sea beyond, but the gale increased in intensity, piling up floes against the shore and compressing the mushy stuff so emphatically that it became like rock. They took refuge on the lee side of one of the bergs, but when at last, several days later, the gale let up a bit, but only a bit, they learned they could not get out. And with the pressure of the pack what it was, they *would* not get out unless and until there was a correspondingly strong gale from the south, to blow all that ice out to sea again.

So there they were. They could not move in any direction. In the words of Orde-Lees, they were stuck "Like an almond in the middle of a chocolate bar."

CHAPTER 16

THE CREW of a vessel previously stalled in the ice of the Weddell Sea did not survive that experience unscarred, their ordeal being featured by what came to be known as the "madhouse promenade." This was the crew of the 1897-1899 expedition in the *Belgica,* commanded by Baron de Gerlache, the man who was to be a partner in the building of the *Endurance.* The leader and the ship were Belgian, as was half the crew, the other half being Norwegian. There was one American, Dr. Cook, who later became famous as the self-styled discoverer of the North Pole. And one of the Norwegians was Roald Amundsen, who actually did discover the South Pole. Both these men were making their first polar voyage, and they became fast friends.

Virtually all of the *Belgica* crew had scurvy; but even worse than scurvy was the horror of the long cold night, the Antarctic winter. Several went mad, literally. One, through hysteria, was deaf and dumb for months. Another kept trying to hide himself because he believed that all the rest were looking for a chance to murder him.

Almost all of them acted strangely, glancing sideways at their neighbors. Officers and seamen alike took to walking around the deck in a wide oval, staying well away from one another in an effort to retain their sanity; and they would keep this up for hours on end until they were so tired that they thought they could sleep. This was the "madhouse promenade."

De Gerlache had not expected to be iced in and was not prepared with medicines, books, heavy clothing, extra fuel oil. Shackleton had, and was.

He made no secret of the seriousness of their predicament, but talked it over openly, many times, with the men. This was the way it was with every problem aboard the *Endurance*. It was not "pure democracy," as in a New England town meeting, for the Boss himself always had the final say; but anybody could be heard.

Anyway, the boss looked upon this as a delay rather than an immediate danger. They would get out of the ice in the spring, and go to South Georgia to refit, and then come back for a second try. It was as simple as that. If Shackleton had any qualms he never let them show.

From time to time, when they saw a lead ahead, the men would get out with axes and picks and try to cut a channel for the ship, attempts that were patently futile. But it was good exercise.

The dogs were taken off deck by means of a canvas chute and housed in dogloos built of ice and packed snow. A great deal of ingenuity went into this work. There were towers, turrets, domes, minarets, even a balcony. The dogloos were located only a few feet from the ship.

Just after they left Grytviken, Shackleton had announced the names of those who would go with him on the dash to the Pole. These were Frank Wild, Tom Crean, Dr. Alexander H. Macklin, Hurley the photographer, and Marston the artist. Each was to make up a team of dogs and train it in his own way. One of them, for instance, instead of employing the customary "Mush!" as a command to start, used to call out "Yoicks, tally ho!" and his dogs understood him just as well. These were not purebred huskies, but a mixed bag from northern Canada, mutts really, nasty among themselves, forever snapping and snarling. Again and again it was necessary to break up fights, and this could not be done by simple command but only by sheer strength. Dr. Macklin used to clip the dogs with an uppercut, a language they understood.

Another thing. If in coursing on a run the dogs saw or smelled a seal or a penguin, they would go berserk. Each wanted to eat the thing, and since the dogs would be in harness, this made it trying on the driver. Nevertheless, force prevailed. The men got harsh, and the dogs accepted that.

Dr. McIlroy drove the sledge and team that would be for Sir Ernest, who never wished to leave the ship for long.

Soon after they were put on the ice, the dogs began to suffer from some strange malady, and 14 of them died. Dr. Macklin and Dr. McIlroy performed autopsies and discovered large red worms, some of them more than a foot long. The other 55 clearly were suffering from the same parasite, but there was nothing that could be done about it. This was not because Shackleton had forgotten to order worm medicine, but because in spite of the order, somebody had failed to check it in, and the stuff simply was not aboard. The balance of the pack, however, survived; and to help offset the losses there were two litters of pups, eight in all.

Frank Hurley, happening to boast that he had the fastest team, was promptly challenged by Frank Wild, and the next day they staged a dog derby, Shackleton acting as starter. They made a field day of it, with banners, binoculars, a bugle, and betting—the bets largely candy bars or cigarettes or pipe tobacco. Wild won.

They even tried training the puppies, hitching them to a sled. It was good for a laugh.

The ice for some distance around the entrapped vessel was free of hummocks or crevasses, so that it was safe to play on. Besides the soccer, they had several hockey matches. They might have forgotten to bring worm medicine, but they had not forgotten their skates. The ice was posted with certain familiar names, to identify landmarks. Thus there was an Embankment, a Trafalgar Square, a Shaftsbury Avenue, and, of course, the racetrack was known as Epsom Downs.

It was January 27th when they really admitted that they were fast, for it was on that day that

Shackleton decreed that for purposes of routine the *Endurance* was no longer a ship but had become a camp. And at the same time he ordered the fires be put out, to save coal.

This resulted in several changes in their activities. Watches were abolished, except that there was a night watchman every night, the men taking turns, Shackleton included. But Shackleton was up and around practically all of the time anyway, so that the seamen often wondered if he ever got any sleep. And there was very little for a hand to do, only two or three hours of regular work a day; the rest of the time they had to fend for themselves.

The hands had a stove in their forecastle, where they were comfortable enough, but the officers and scientists had been sleeping in cabins in the deckhouse right over the boiler room, and when the fires were doused these cabins became unbearably cold. So they switched things around. The supplies that had been stored in the main hold—a rectangular chamber 35 by 25 feet, with a six-foot ceiling clearance—were shifted to the deckhouse and to such coal bunkers as were empty, while the scientists and officers took over the hold. The carpenter built them a table and some chairs there, from empty crates, and they had a stove. He also built individual cubbyhole bunks around the walls. This was called The Ritz.

In his own cubicle just off the Ritz, Sir Ernest kept the ship's library. An omnivorous reader himself, he was always prepared to discuss the merits of a book of prose or poetry when it was returned.

In the beginning there were many seals and penguins to kill, and kill them the explorers did, by the score, so that on April 10th, Shackleton could estimate they had stored away 5,000 pounds of meat and blubber, or enough to last for three months without recourse to their canned fuel and canned food. After that the animals were scarcer, for they were moving north to get away from the awful oncoming Antarctic winter.

Though it looked stationary, since nothing about it stirred, the ship itself also was moving. It drifted south and west for a little while until it got to the 77th parallel of latitude, at 35 degrees west longitude. This was the farthest south it reached, only about 60 miles from Vahsel Bay.

There was no dream of pushing for those 60 miles. Such a distance across unknown ice, with the untried dogs, moving many hundreds of tons of supplies, would be unthinkable. It was too late for any dash this year anyway; it was February 22nd. And leave the ship? How? Who would organize a relief party?

After that they began to move more west-northwest, as expected. It was the normal Weddell Sea ice pack clockwise journey. They would probably edge farther and farther west and north, until they were in the crook of the elbow of the Antarctica Peninsula, where the crush would be greatest, the pressure most severe. Would the *Endurance* survive that?

Early in March, they turned west-northwest, rolling without effort.

In April the movement changed to due north-west.

After all, they were starting home, if only at the rate of three or four miles a day.

CHAPTER 17

LEONARD D. A. HUSSEY, an immensely likable young man, was in an awkward position. He was a meteorologist without any stones.

Fresh out of Cambridge, where he had majored in anthropology, he had so much wished to be taken on the expedition that he promised to study meteorology furiously in the few weeks that remained; and Shackleton, who liked his looks, had agreed. Hussey did a fine job, too, in the time at his command; but what good did that do him aboard the *Endurance,* which never touched land?

It might have been Frank Wild who gave him a little something to work with, an excuse for his notebooks and his microscope. Wild was, by common consent the chief hunter of the crew, a crack shot. When the game got scarce, Worsley, who had the best eyes, would post himself in the crow's nest and spot seals or penguins in the distance, beasts that Wild, below, could not have seen even with glasses; and Worsley would start the hunter in the right direction. The seals were mostly crabeaters or Weddells, the latter a species that could run up to 400 pounds. The Emperor penguins were the biggest kind, as much as four feet tall.

Now, pebbles are important to a penguin, any kind of penguin. They hoard them; they steal them from one another; they trade them; and, for reasons best known to themselves, they use them in their mating ceremonies. It seems that they also, perhaps inadvertently, sometimes swallow them. In any event, when cutting-up time came for the birds Frank Wild had bagged, tiny stones often were found in their stomachs. These were turned over to Leonard D. A. Hussey, who examined them closely.

It was not much, but it was better than nothing.

An older and much less sociable scientist was James M. Wordie, a dour Scot, the geologist of the party. Periodically he lowered over the side a lead can in which he scooped up samples of the sea bottom; and these he would study. One day some of the boys intercepted that can on its way back and filled it with macaroni. Wordie never said a word. He was not molested again, for there would be no profit in playing pranks on a person like that.

Frank Hurley took scads of pictures, and when the closing down of the Great Night limited this activity to flash work, he easily became the unofficial chief electrician, stringing up floodlights. In addition to these, Shackleton caused to be rigged on the surrounding ice a series of outleading wires by means of which a person who had strayed too far from the ship could find his way back.

Marston sketched and painted. He was volatile, as many artists are. One moment he would be bubbling over with playful ideas and practical jokes, and the next he would be brooding about his wife and three children.

The dogs were tended by their separate drivers, though now and then the night watchman would go down to check the dogloos, just to make sure that everything was all right.

Tom Crean had charge of the sledges and kept them in perfect condition just in case they should ever be needed.

The third officer, Alfred Cheetham, was in general charge of the men—under Shackleton, of course.

The stowaway, Percy Blackboro, no longer was thought of as a stowaway. He fitted in beautifully, young, strong, willing, well liked.

The hardest ones to find work for, at this stage of the expedition, were the first and second engineers, respectively Louis Rickinson and A. J. Kerr, and the two firemen, Ernest Holness and William Stevenson.

One who never moped for lack of work was Charles J. Green, the cook. A squeaking wisp of a man with no sense of humor, he was generally believed to have, in the phrase of the time, "bats in his belfry;" but if he didn't joke, neither did he complain, and in the galley he was a star-spangled wonder. To say that he worked from dawn to sundown would mean nothing, those

119

phenomena being absent now, but it was certain that he put in 12 or 14 hours a day.

With the decline of hunting and the blotting-out of dog-train coursing—for besides the drivers the sledges carried passengers as ballast to simulate cargo—it was up to the individual men to find their own exercise procedures. This they did in accordance with their own wishes. There was never, however, anything even remotely resembling the "madhouse promenade" of the *Belgica*.

The less physical pastimes were held generally in the Ritz. There was a passion, at first, for guessing games: "I am N, a famous general." "Did you win the battle of Austerlitz?" "No, I am not Napoleon." Things like that.

Often their haircutting sessions were hilarious. Customarily they clowned it. One day or night— they were the same—they cut *all* their hair off, after which they had their picture taken. That picture has not survived, which perhaps is just as well. They must have looked superlatively silly.

Like prisoners of war they seized the opportunity to instruct and learn from one another. Thus, Frank Hurley lectured on Australia, Dr. McIlroy on Malaya, Frank Worsley on New Zealand.

They held a mock trial, almost everybody participating.

As at Cape Royds they used every excuse for a celebration, one of their biggest, a real fete, being held on the night of Midwinter's Day, June 22nd. That had been the shortest day of the year, lasting only a few minutes.

Even in the forecastle there were no pin-up pictures of naked women. The men themselves never undressed beyond their underwear, and they seldom even mentioned sex. It was easier that way. An exception was Dr. McIlroy, a handsome, much-traveled man with a gay-bachelor background; but even he, though he might sometimes allude to a past conquest, as a rule avoided the subject.

That same Dr. McIlroy and Shackleton himself, having failed in repeated attempts to get others to learn the new game of auction bridge, or, as it was sometimes called, Bath Club bridge, a refinement of bridge whist, resorted to sundry forms of two-handed or honeymoon bridge, none of which was satisfactory. There was, of course, a great deal of checkers and chess playing, and many games of tic-tac-toe were played.

They were snug enough aboard the *Endurance,* and the weather was unexpectedly quiet, though barometer and thermometer alike kept going down. On July 14th, for instance, the barometric pressure hit 28.88, an all-time low; there was a great deal of snow, and wind from the southwest. The temperature dropped to 34 degrees below.

They were still drifting, as they determined by taking repeated shots of the sun whenever it presented itself, but the ice around them—and it was principally the ice that they worried about—was comparatively free of cracks. It was not so in the distance, which presented a turbulent sur-

face. As early as June, Frank Worsley, that inde-
fatigable diarist, recorded:

"The noise was very loud, like an enormous
train with squeaky axles being shunted with
much bumping and clattering. Mingled with
this were the sound of steamer's whistles starting to blow, cocks crowing and, underfoot,
moans and groans of damned souls in torment.
A constant undertone as of a heavy, distant surf
is heard whenever the louder noises decrease
or cease for a moment."

The pressure was terrific. The white Stone-
henge caused by uptilted slabs of ice was getting
closer all the time. Sooner or later, unless they
could get out of there, it would engulf them.

CHAPTER 18

THAT MIDWINTER'S DAY of 1915, June 22nd, marked a turning point. Thereafter they could expect the light to last longer, and maybe soon they would be able to get in another game of soccer.

The day itself had been dark and very noisy. One bang in particular made them jump. It was louder than the loudest cannon, and it seemed nearby. They hurried out on the ice with lanterns, and they found a crack several feet wide, a southwest-northeast crack, only 300 yards from the port bow of the *Endurance*. Could this mean that the ice was about to break up? They watched that crack anxiously. The next day it widened a little, but after that it closed and was seen no more.

A few days later there was a terrible southwest blow that caused the vessel to list six degrees to port. The boats were cleared; the dogs were hurried aboard—the men had staged drills for just this purpose—but the dogs' houses, on the starboard side, those baroque ice mansions upon which so much skill and loving care had been spent—were wrecked. The attack, by huge masses of tumbling ice, came from the starboard side. It lasted only about an hour, but that was a terrifying hour. The ship was fairly bombarded by huge chunks of ice, so that she shuddered and screamed like a thing in pain. The rudder was forced out of position, but no other serious harm was done, and afterward she righted herself.

Peary's *Roosevelt,* like Nansen's (and later Amundsen's) sturdy little *Fram,* had a round bottom and was of very shallow draft. The idea was that if caught in the ice, the vessel would be hoisted to the surface and lie on her side, rather than resist and be crushed. *Endurance* had been built somewhat along these lines, though she was a deeper vessel with more of a V-bottom. She might be forced up instead of being crushed, but such a position would only expose that much more surface to the tumbling, relentless boulders of ice. Nothing like these Weddell Sea conditions obtained in the Arctic.

On August 29th there was another long crack, and the men took heart. They also took pickaxes, and they toiled mightily, and they hoisted sail, for there was clear water not far away. *Endurance* didn't move an inch.

The days kept getting longer, and the temperature rose. On September 10th they had a heat wave when the mercury soared to two degrees *above* zero.

There was a second and much more severe attack on the night of August 31st, when for hours on end they thought that they must be splintered, and the noise was such that nobody could sleep. Yet they survived, somehow.

There was another one-hour intense assault on September 30th, in the middle of the afternoon. They scurried up on deck, convinced that they were lost at last; and when they went below again it was to find that thick oaken beams had been bent like bamboo and everything was at least a little out of whack—but the ship still was afloat.

"All hands are watching and standing by," Worsley recorded in his diary, "but to our relief, just as it appears she can stand no more, the huge floe weighing possibly a million tons or more yields to our little ship by cracking across, ¼ of a mile, and so relieves the pressure. The behavior of our ship in the ice has been magnificent. Undoubtedly she is the finest little wooden vessel ever built."

Many of the others felt that way too, gaining confidence in the gallant craft that had stood up so well to three savage storms.

She was blown far to port again October 18th, a list of about 30 degrees, and she remained there, for the ice blocks were piled against her starboard side. This made it inconvenient for the men to move about, above as well as below. The carpenter, irascible little McNeish, built slats on the deck to help them and to help the dogs.

The day after that, Shackleton ordered the fires to be lighted again, so that in case the ice did break up they would give the *Endurance* a chance to make a try for open water. The previous time they had been obliged to depend upon their canvas. It was good to see smoke at the stubby funnel again, even though it was thin stuff, for they had eked out the precious coal by mixing it with wood and blubber.

The ship had righted itself by this time, and they were back on regular ship's watches, four hours on, four off, seamen and officers alike, except that Shackleton, in Worsley's words, "retained the privilege of being up all the time."

On October 22nd the wind backed around from due southwest to due northeast, and this was bad, very bad, for it greatly increased the pressure as it drove more and more ice against the *Endurance,* pushing her into the elbow crook of the Antarctic Peninsula, so that the open sea they yearned for was farther away than ever.

On October 24th she began to leak. Ice had clawed away part of the sternpost. They had a hand pump, a Downton, but this was ludicrously inadequate, and they tried the bilge pumps in the engine room, where they still had some steam. No water came up. The intakes below, far down near the keel, must have become frozen.

Three men went down there where, knee-deep in blubber-soaked coal, they labored for an hour with hot water and a blow torch, expecting that every minute would be their last. They finally got the pumps cleared.

Meanwhile McNeish, who though testy was a furious worker and prepared, it would seem, for just about every possible emergency, had started to construct a coffer dam in the engine room in the hope of confining the water to the extreme stern. Several seamen helped him to caulk this— it was made mostly of boards—with strips of old blanket. Others worked the hand pumps or got material ashore. The three lifeboats were put over, onto the ice. The dogs slithered down their canvas chute. Ordinarily this experience would have sent them into a frenzy of excitement, but today they seemed to sense that the end was near at hand, and they were quiet. Supplies were carried out to the ice.

All that night they labored, and when at seven o'clock in the morning Shackleton called a one-hour halt, most of the men were so muscle-weary that they could not go to sleep. Green was ready with hot porridge. Then they went back to work, all that day, all that night. . . .

The dogs were hitched to the sledges and the sledges loaded with supplies, so that everything would be ready for a quick getaway in case the *Enduranco,* in going down, would so split the ice at this point as to make it uninhabitable.

For she was going down. There was no question in anybody's mind about that. The only problem was how to keep her afloat long enough to enable the men to get most of the portable supplies ashore.

McNeish's coffer dam, on which he had worked constantly for 28 hours, was a wonderful jury job, but the pumps just weren't big enough to keep up with the leak. The water that did get in found its way below and forward, and it froze there, in the bow, which soon dipped. The sternpost and the rudder had by this time been carried completely away.

The *Endurance*, screaming horribly (they all had that same feeling that they were witnessing the death of some great animal), was being squeezed to death.

Frank Wild looked at the Boss, and the Boss nodded.

"She's going, boys," Wild said. "It's time to get off and walk."

They had a last meal aboard, a spread, one of Green's best, though they were too spent to appreciate it.

Water was swishing around their ankles, and the mess-room clock still was ticking on the wall, though canted at a crazy angle, when they went out.

CHAPTER 19

THERE WAS no panic. They were too tired for anything like that. They had five tents, all pale green. Two of these were conventional center-pole types; the other three, the invention of George Marston the artist, were a raised-hoop type that was easier to pitch, though it was to prove not as firm against the gales. The three Marston tents were filled with sleeping men before the other two had been fully raised. All anybody could think of was sleep.

Everybody, that is, except Sir Ernest Henry Shackleton. *He* could not sleep at such a time. He prowled the camp like a lost soul, a ghost.

It was as well that he did. There was a sharp cracking sound that seemed to come from right under his feet, and when he looked down he saw a crevasse snaking right through the center of the camp, which might at any moment become two separate camps, floating far apart. He awakened the others, and hustled them, grumbling, leaden-eyed, to a safer spot a short distance away, where they went right to sleep again.

Shackleton always believed in a good hot

breakfast. It could make all the difference, he thought. With the dawn he and Hurley and Wild climbed aboard the half-submerged *Endurance*, rescued some milk, and boiled this over an improvised stove made from the binnacle. Then they took it to the camp and carried it from tent to tent, dishing out individual portions as an eye-opener. They had gone to a lot of trouble to do this, and it was annoying to hear some of the boys grumble when they were served.

"If any of you gentlemen would like your boots cleaned," Frank Wild said, "just leave them outside."

It earned him a laugh, and this was good; a favorable way to start life on the ice.

They christened the camp Camp Dump because it looked like a dump, as indeed it was, being littered with all manner of bags and boxes and bales, tools and gear, rigging, planking, anything grab-up-able. It was located about 200 yards from the starboard bow of the wreck of the *Endurance*, the bowsprit and jib-boom of which had fallen off with a very loud crash heard only by the pacing Boss, just before dawn.

They took stock, these 28 marooned men.

The *Endurance* had been imprisoned in the ice for more than nine months—January 18th to October 27th—and it was now utterly lost to them, since no prodigies of seamanship could have kept it afloat and in motion, even if no ice had been there; indeed, just now it was only the ice that was holding it up. They figured their position to be 69 degrees five minutes south, 51 degrees 30 minutes west, which meant that they were almost 500 miles—in a straight line—from the point off the Luitold Coast where they had lost control of their vessel. However, the *Endurance,* blown by the winds and carried by unseen currents, had not traveled in a straight line, but rather in a line—for they had worked it out on papers—all zigs and zags; so that it was estimated that she had in fact gone more than 1,500 miles at the compulsion of wind and wave.

They had the bottom of the world pretty much to themselves. They were about 1,200 miles from the southernmost outpost of civilization, that same little whaling station of Grytviken in South Georgia where they had coaled, and the intervening space was all unpredictable ice floes and wild, wild sea. They were about that same distance, 1,200 miles, from the South Pole, a place they now knew they would never reach.

Nobody knew that they were there, except in a very general way. It was not likely that any relief expedition would be sent to look for them for at least another two years, if then, and the possibility of such an expedition finding them in that flat wilderness where they had no means of signaling was so small as to be infinitesimal.

They had had a small wireless set, but it was not strong enough to reach anything. Neither could they receive anything, not even the periodic Morse Code time signals sent out from southern South America in order to enable them to correct their chronometers, if correction was needed.

The inner or eastern coast of the Antarctic Peninsula was not far away, but what if they did get there. How would that benefit them? It was north that they wanted to go. They wanted to get out of polar waters. And assuredly they would have to do this by themselves. Nobody was going to come and help them.

It was Shackleton's belief that their best bet would be to make for Paulet Island, which was north-by-northwest of their present position, a distance of about 350 miles. Paulet was uninhabited, a tiny frozen place off the end of the Antarctic Peninsula—in other words off the extreme northern tip of the continent of Antarctica—but it was well stocked with food and fuel for polar explorers. Shackleton happened to know this because when he was in Britain after being sent back by Scott from the *Discovery* expedition he was consulted as an expert about sending a relief ship to rescue the crew of the wrecked Nordenskjiold expedition ship, who had spent two torturous years in the Weddell Sea ice. At that time, as a part of the operation, an emergency supply had been left, well-housed, on Paulet. The crew had been rescued, but the supply was still there, as Shackleton knew. They might reach it. What would happen after that, to be sure, was anybody's guess.

He had an alternative plan. Snow Hill Island was an even smaller and more barren spot, a little south of Paulet. It was near the mainland, to which, almost undoubtedly, even in the summer, it was connected by ice, so that they could cross.

They could make camp on the mainland, and a selected group of them, the better climbers, could scale the glacier to Wilhelmina Bay on the west coast of the peninsula. Whalers often put into Wilhelmina Bay, which was normally clear of ice in the summer. If they waited long enough there somebody was sure to come along, and a relief party could be formed. In preparation for this feat of climbing, Shackleton ordered that screws be fastened to the soles of four pairs of boots.

They were drifting toward both those islands, Snow Hill and Paulet, as the navigators, Captain Worsley and the physicist, Reginald James, assured them.

By the time they were ready to start, the seals and penguins would be back—and indeed they were killing them already, the first fresh food they had eaten in five months—and they could stock up their twelve sleds and three boats with this and with whatever they could save from the sinking *Endurance*.

They swarmed over the *Endurance* carefully, for her very deck was awash now, and she might go at any moment. They drove a hole in the galley roof and fished up many cases of provisions. They fastened a blue Union Jack to her highest bit of standing spars, so that when she did go down it would be with colors flying. It was the least they could do for a gallant lady.

They saved all the canvas they could for tent-patching. They hauled off a large pile of boards, out of which the carpenter worked all the nails. Nails could be useful. The rock samples and bottom samples, such as these were, had been irretrievably lost, but two of the forecastle hands came upon Hurley's photographic plates, a great find. The plates were made of heavy glass, and they could not all be taken, for on the trip to come every ounce would count, but Shackleton and Hurley himself looked them over one by one and as soon as they had decided against a plate they smashed it, lest they be tempted to change their minds.

The third day on the ice Shackleton harangued the men. He told them frankly that their chances were not too good. He stressed the need for stripping to absolute essentials. Each man had been issued heavy clothing, a sleeping bag, a pannikin, a knife, a spoon; but of additional belongings, personal property, he could only carry two pounds. There were exceptions. Those who were maintaining diaries could take them along. The two physicians of course had their medicine chests. Chippy McNeish was allowed, besides his two pounds, all the tools that he had been able to save, which was not many. And Hussey the meteorologist was commanded to cling to his banjo, though it weighed twelve pounds, case included. That instrument had long ago proved its usefulness.

Shackleton waxed dramatic. He threw a handful of golden sovereigns on the ice, as though to indicate that gold wasn't about to do them any good where they were going. He threw down a gold watch and chain. Then he did something that caused them to gasp. From under his parka he drew the Bible that Queen Alexandra herself had given him as a farewell gift, surely his most treasured possession. He tore out only the flyleaf on which she had written "the 23rd Psalm," and that page of Job (his favorite book) which contained the quotation: "Out of whose womb came the ice? and the hoary frost of heaven, who hath gendered it?" The rest of that precious Bible he laid on the ice, alongside of the watch and chain, the gold coins. And he walked away.

It was effective. All the rest of that day men were, with sighs, relinquishing beloved articles too heavy to take. By sunset—and the sun was not setting until about nine o'clock these days— there was a large pile.

Next morning, before he and Wild started north as an advance party to hack some manner of trail for the sledges, Shackleton issued another order. The four weakest puppies, unable to pull their weight, must be killed. The other four, under First Officer Greenstreet, were almost as strong as their parents. Also Mrs. Chippy, the carpenter's cat (really a tomcat, but by the time McNeish had learned his mistake he decided to stick by it), had to go.

This order was obeyed.

The way was rough. The snow was half melted; and pulling the boats and the sledges, the men complained, was like hauling them through mud. Shackleton and Wild had cut miniature mountain passes through some of the snow-ice ridges, as tall as two-story houses, but others had to be surmounted, and it was agonizing, back-breaking work, done mostly in relays, the men pulling as well as the dogs, the men leaning over so that their faces almost scraped the snow.

That first day they progressed scarcely a mile. The second day they did barely more than half of that, and they were exhausted.

It was enough. It was too much. The Boss was not planning to kill his men right away. He decreed that since they were now on a sound, thick floe, they would stay there until the conditions changed, as they surely would soon. So they pitched camp. They called this depot Camp Ocean.

Shackleton personally made the tent assignments, making sure that there was one reliable aide of his in each, and that no two potential troublemakers would be put together. This was the most telling time of all, right now, as he well knew. The big thing was to keep the men busy, to establish regular duties.

So night watchmen were appointed. Hunting parties were organized. The dog-sled superintendents renewed their exercise runs. Again and again small groups were sent on foot to what miraculously remained of the *Endurance,* and they brought back all sorts of odds and ends that could just as well be left at Camp Ocean as at the nearby Camp Dump.

Among these things were books, which was good because there was so much daylight for reading now, and cards. The Boss usually had a game of poker in progress in his own tent, number one, which he shared with Dr. McIlroy and three others, and this attracted a certain amount of attention, of off-hour interest. Gradually these kibitzers were talked into taking some auction-bridge lessons, and in very little time a mania for bridge swept the camp. The men were crazy about it. They played every time they got a chance.

The sport was interrupted November 6th, by a raging blizzard from the southwest. It was the first such storm that most of the men had endured out on the ice, and it allowed little freedom for doubles and slams and such, but they loved it all the same, for it was blowing from the right direction and would help to move them on their way.

"We all hope it blows for a month," McNeish wrote in his diary.

It blew for just about 48 hours; but every little bit helped.

The salvagers had taken apart the deckhouse, and this was carried by dog train to Camp Ocean, where it was reassembled as a general supply house. Near it, in the middle of the camp, there was a wooden lookout tower, its purpose being not to spot relief vessels—which would have been absurd—but to spot seals. Worsley was standing near this tower on the afternoon of November 21st, about ten minutes to five when the Boss, nearby, pointed and, yelled, "There she goes!"

Worsley ran up the ladder, and, sure enough there she did go—the gallant *Endurance*. She shivered, tilted, all that was left of her. And then the bow went under, and the stern rose perhaps 20 feet into the air, straight up, and hung a moment, before sliding out of sight. Ice closed over the small black hole that was left, completely obliterating it. The whole thing had taken only ten minutes.

"I cannot write about it," was what Sir Ernest told his diary that night.

CHAPTER 20

THE CLASSIC ANSWER to the question "What one book would you take with you to a desert island, provided you could take only one?" is, of course: "Howland's Manual of Small-Boat Building." Chippy McNeish would not have needed this. He never used a ruler. He would stare at a slot for a moment, and then cut or saw or plane a piece to fit into it; and fit that piece *would*, exactly. McNeish was not popular, for he was a surly brute and puritanical, wincing at profanity; but he was generously admired.

Early in what the men sometimes playfully called the Ice Age, the carpenter approached the Boss with a suggestion that he build a sloop, a real seagoing vessel big enough to carry all of them and all their supplies. He would do this, he said, by knocking apart their three boats, two cutters, and an undecked whaler, and reassembling these in one, together with certain other planks and pieces of wood that had been saved from the *Endurance*.

It was a bold, imaginative plan, and Shackleton, who like the others had faith in McNeish, gave it deep consideration. He finally decided against it, because, he said, such a vessel, even without a load, would be too clumsy to haul over the kind of ice field they would have to cross before they reached open water. With the coming of summer, the leads, or channels of open water, would surely increase in number and perhaps also in width. The small boats could utilize these leads for sailing, when they went in the right direction, thus giving the men a rest; but the leads would only be obstacles to the sort of boat McNeish proposed. No, the Boss would rather have three small ones than one big one. But—couldn't they be strengthened?

They could; and McNeish set to work promptly, with an occasional assist, on request, from a few others: they were all more or less handymen. He raised the sides of all three. He caulked the seams with candlewick mixed in oil paints from George Marston's kit. He painted the boats with seals' blood, which ordinarily would have been fed to the dogs.

Razors and shaving soap could not be considered necessities, and hot water was simply out of the question, so such men as had not already grown beards—about half of them—did so now, at Ocean Camp. It is a ticklish, irritating process for the first week or so, hard on the nerves and even on the fingernails. Moreover, the beards soon got exceedingly dirty.

There were—and still are—among polar explorers two schools of thought about washing the face and beard. Some say it is better to keep them as clean as is convenient, using snow or melted ice. Others contend that the dirt toughens the skin of the face and helps to prevent frostbite.

There is no dust in Antarctica, there are no insects there. How, then, could the men get dirty? It was the blubber smoke.

There are no trees in Antarctica either. Aboard the *Endurance*—back in those dear dead days beyond recall, when they had lived, as they knew now, in the lap of luxury—they had heated their stoves, cooked their food, and stoked their furnaces with coal. The coal had gone to the bottom of the sea, and wood was much too precious a substance to be used as fuel. So blubber was burned.

Blubber is stinky, spitty stuff, and it gives off a thick black smoke. It sooted every exposed surface. There was no escape from it. Happily, Frank Hurley had been obliged to leave his camera behind, so that he could not take their picture. They must have looked like a bevy of baboons, each with a doormat fastened to his chin.

The boats were completed November 26th, and Shackleton called them *James Caird, Dudley Docker,* and *Stancomb-Wills,* after his principal sponsors. The *Caird* was the whaler.

Since it might be necessary to leave the weakest, the *Stancomb-Wills,* behind—depending upon the weather and ice conditions when they set sail—Shackleton assigned not only three-boat but also two-boat positions and commands. This was characteristic of his thoroughness. He had also assigned positions and responsibilities in case the floe upon which they floated went to pieces. Each man knew what was expected of him, and to make sure that he did not forget, the Boss called a drill, unannounced, every now and then.

On December 21st, Shackleton, being impatient, took off on an exploratory trip to the north with Wild, Crean, and Hurley and two of the dog teams. They decided, afterward, that for six miles at least the going would be good; the ice was passable, if just. They decided at the same time to break camp. The next day, December 22nd, they decreed, would arbitrarily be Christmas, and would be celebrated as such. The celebration finished, they would start north.

The men were awakened at 3:30 the next morning. It was fully light by that time, for the days were very long now. The sledges and the boats were loaded. The dogs were harnessed. Then everybody sat down to a feast.

That stingy storekeeper, the ex-Marine physical culture instructor, Orde-Lees, "the belly burglar," who was obsessed by fears of starvation, was forced to disgorge such a stock of foodstuffs it must have pained him greatly. They had in fact much the same menu they'd had at Christmas a year before, when they were still trying to get south to the Antarctic Circle, as they were now striving to get north to it. They had pickles and peaches, ham, sausage, and—again, jugged hare. It was an occasion.

"Curious Christmas. Thoughts of home," the Boss wrote in his diary.

That night they set forth. It was Shackleton's plan to travel at night, sleeping in the daytime, an old desert trick. The reason, as in the desert, was the heat. As midsummer approached, the air became intolerably not-cold in the middle of the day, the temperature going even above the freezing point sometimes for a little while. To men who were swathed in extra-heavy clothes and who by means of shoulder-and-chest harnesses were hauling thousands of pounds of supplies through thick, gluelike slush, this was all but unbearable. The nights, on the other hand, were amiably cool, and it was easy to keep the course, once this had been set, since except for a little while around twelve o'clock it was broad daylight.

They did leave the *Stancomb-Wills* behind, and they left behind as well a large supply of food. They agreed that the going would be hard enough without trying to haul every ounce of supplies.

The going *was* hard. Slush and broken ice and frequent high-pressure ridges made every inch an agony. Nor could they get much rest, even when they crawled into their sleeping bags, for their clothing was at all times wet and they had no changes—except shoes and mittens—and because they had left their wooden tent floors behind, they were obliged to lie on the bare ice, which tended to melt under the heat of their bodies.

There were very few seals, though they had hoped for many. The surrounding ice was worse than it had been at Ocean Camp, and they were in danger all the time of being split up, cast adrift.

There were some mutterings, unheard until this time; and one man, the carpenter, Harry McNeish, revolted. He flatly refused to obey an order given to him by Worsley, who was in charge of hauling the boats, the severest job of all. McNeish contended that according to international maritime usage, when a vessel was sunk the members of its crew had no further obligations to the master. Therefore, he wouldn't pull any more.

Shackleton was called, and, deeply shocked, he took McNeish aside and gave him a long, low, careful talk.

Sir Ernest was a complete egotist, and when any of his orders were not endorsed one hundred percent, he esteemed this disloyalty, even sacrilege. He was shaken. Did any of the other men feel the same way McNeish felt? The carpenter, to be sure, at 56 was by far the oldest of the party. The mean age was less than half that. Would McNeish's protest spread? Shackleton called all the men together. He reread to them the articles of enlistment that they had signed in Buenos Aires. He granted that a seaman's fealty was supposed to cease once a ship had been wrecked—and so did his pay. This, he contended, was an exceptional case. He believed that they were still, in the meaning of the articles, "on board." That is, they were still drawing their pay, though he did not put this into so many words.

144

They remained under his command. Didn't they concur with this? Nobody disputed him, though McNeish continued to sulk.

However, when a further advance was called, without a word, McNeish got back into his harness.

What else could he have done? His one-man mutiny was no more than a fit of nerves, a cracking-up. He could not possibly set off by himself, when he had no navigating instruments, and if he simply stayed where he was, refusing to follow, assuming that Shackleton would permit such a course, he would soon be dead—a matter of days. So he plugged on.

Shackleton never forgave him.

December 29 they settled down on a floe in what they called Mark Time Camp. They were utterly miserable, and could hardly stand. They wished, if not aloud, that they had never left Ocean Camp. In five days of backbreaking labor they had gone only nine miles, and they were worse off than ever—much worse.

New Year's Eve passed cheerlessly. There was no champagne. There were no noisemakers. The men were getting hungry.

After a few days, fearing that the floe would break underneath them, they floundered and slid to another one not far away, and there, on January 14th, they made a camp that they called Patience Camp.

It was a good name.

CHAPTER 21

THIS WAS the dreariest time. A show of routine was maintained, but it was only a show; and in truth there was not enough work to keep one man busy, let alone 28. They were on an ice floe roughly round and about a mile across, but the surface was slushy and hummocky, so that they could not have played hockey or soccer even if they still had the puck and the ball. There was no longer any hunting, never a seal or a penguin. There were no more exercise runs or dog derbies, because there were no more dogs.

The second day at Patience Camp, Shackleton ordered Wild, McIlroy, Marston, and Crean to do away with their dogs. This was not for eating purposes but to save on the fodder. The rest of the trip, it was patent, would be aquatic. The dogs would have to be destroyed sooner or later, and it might come about, with the absence of game, that the men would need their pemmican.

Hurley's and Macklin's dogs he would save for awhile to bring supplies from Ocean Camp, which was only about eight miles away.

Frank Wild was the executioner. He squatted

behind a ridge of hummocks, his revolver in his hand, and the dogs were led up to him one by one; each got a bullet through the brain. They were altogether unsuspecting, for they had learned to know and to love these men, their masters; nor did the sounds of the shots in any way frighten those who awaited their turns. They died with their tails wagging, every one. Afterward the heaped carcasses were covered with snow, lest the other dogs, when they returned from Ocean Camp, go wild with the smell.

Hurley and Macklin, together with their teams, made the trip to Ocean Camp usually at night, which for purposes of light was the same as the day. It was a rugged trip, all soft, wet snow and thin, jagged ice, so that the huskies again and again broke through to their bellies, and their paws were cut. The poor beasts were given a meal and two and a half hours' rest at Ocean, which was largely under water, while Macklin and Hurley loaded the two sledges with some 500 pounds of food. The trip back was almost as bad. They could follow their own tracks, but they were pulling a great deal more. Macklin's lead dog, Bos'n, vomited, and several of the others were limping. When they did get back to Patience Camp, they were dead-beat, and they slumped down in the slush, not even yammering to be fed, as ordinarily they would do. They did not know that they were doomed.

The floe was getting smaller, as it was chipped away on all sides by other floes, but they had no thought of moving. Theirs was still the best in sight. And so they went "hurtling along," as Worsley put it, "at two miles a day."

The slaughter of the dogs was resented by some of the men, who understandably were edgy. Also, it was an act that smacked of desperation.

Even more depressing was the lack of anything to do. "God, send us open water soon, or we shall go balmy," Greenstreet wrote in his diary. There were no more mock trials, no more costume parties, and every now and then, for all their efforts, a snarl broke through the surface.

The supply of blubber being low, they were cut to one hot meal a day, and that was not piping. Whether it was the seal meat or the uncooked pemmican or something else, most of the men were noisy with flatulence and had diarrhea. This, to be sure, *did* give them something to do; but it was something that they did not enjoy doing, behind a hummock to get out of the cold wind, especially now that there was no more toilet paper.

The wind came mostly from the south, but when it did come from the north, it was a cold wind. This was disquieting, because it indicated that the ice pack stretched for many miles north of them and that the open sea was far away. A wind that had been blowing over the open sea would be warmer.

North wind or south, they continued to drift north, as did all the ice around them. They watched this ice night and day, for they were never out of danger. Besides the floes, there were always at least a few bergs in sight, mountains of ice, and these, being so deep in the sea, obeying unseen currents, would sometimes seem to go crazy, changing direction suddenly and picking up speed. Should one of these maverick bergs hit the floe on which Camp Patience rested, it would mean the end of the expedition.

Their course was constantly north, but it was not often *dead* north. Sometimes they went a bit west, which was what they wanted, but at other times they tended to drift a little east, away from the mainland. If they missed those tiny islands off the tip of the Antarctic Peninsula, they would surely starve.

A great gale from the south struck them, and for almost a week it blew hard. It was accompanied by a wet, nasty snow, which made things highly uncomfortable; but still they were delighted. Let it blow!

When it had cleared and the sun had come out and Worsley could get a sight, he announced that they had passed the Antarctic Circle. They had gone 84 miles north in the six days of storm. They had also gone 15 miles east, but less mention was made of this. They were not much more than 150 miles from Paulet.

Hurley's dogs were killed, then Macklin's and Crean's; only the puppies were still alive.

Fog enshrouded the party for two days. It came from the north, and it felt and smelled like a proper sea fog, which would suggest open water not far away. They snatched at every hope, they were so bored.

149

Worsley, who had the best eyes in the outfit, climbed the highest hummock on the floe—about 60 feet, with a pair of binoculars; and when he came down it was to announce that the Ocean Camp floe was still behind them, and that, no doubt because of the storm, it was nearer—only about five miles away now. Also, the ice conditions between the two floes were much better.

This news brought an immediate resumption of pleas to the Boss that a party be sent back to fetch the third boat, the *Stancomb-Wills*. It was still there; Worsley had seen it through the glasses.

Shackleton hummed. He did not like to be pushed. He thought it over for a couple of days before he gave his permission.

This was work for men, not dogs. February 2nd, soon after midnight, a party of 18, headed by Wild, sallied forth. While they were gone Shackleton worried about them, as he always worried and fretted when any of his men were out of sight, and when at last they were seen returning, he went to meet them with a kettle of tea.

They had enjoyed clear trudging, no trouble at all; but when the next day Shackleton sent out Worsley, Macklin, and Crean with the rest of the dogs attached to two sledges, for the purpose of bringing back more supplies from Ocean Camp, they encountered leads that were too wide to jump, so they returned empty-handed.

Day after drab day dragged along, and those

days were getting shorter, and still there' was no open water in sight.

February 17th they awakened to find twenty-odd Adélie penguins not far from the camp, on the same floe. They were low on ammunition, so they seized every sort of cudgel they could find—oars, axes, whatnot—and steathily surrounded the unsuspecting fowl. The penguin, with its absurd, stubby little wings, cannot fly, but it can move across the ice mighty fast by tobogganing on its chest, and once it reaches water, it is a swift swimmer. None of these escaped.

Next day there were hundreds more. This was obviously a mass migration. No doubt the birds planned to stop on the floe for only a short while, a drastic miscalculation on their part. By the time the last of them flipped away, on February 24th, the men had killed almost 600.

This was not the bonanza it may seem. The Adélie—named after the wife of a French Antarctic explorer—is the smallest of the various kinds of penguins. Its liver is praised as a delicacy, but there isn't much meat on its body, and even less blubber.

Still, the catch did stave off immediate starvation, which they had feared. The tea and the cocoa were all gone, and there was very little powdered milk left. When they craved a drink of water they had to fill a tobacco tin with snow and take this into a sleeping bag for a while; and even then it yielded only a couple of skimpy teaspoonfuls. Most of the men sucked ice.

151

On March 9th there was a series of swells that made them believe that their floe—only about 200 feet across now—was about to dissolve. They struck the tents and manned the boats. But the floe held, and the jagged ice stayed packed around it as tight as ever.

On March 16th they used up the last of the flour. Thereafter they had only some form of meat to eat. Starving men traditionally are supposed to dream of thick juicy steaks. These castaways did not. They dreamed of omelets, cucumbers, vegetable marrow, spicy rather than sweet dishes; but they never wanted to see another piece of meat.

They sighted land on March 23rd. This was an oceanic flyspeck that was identified as one of the Danger Islets. It was far away, and clearly unattainable even if it had been worth attaining. But it *was* land, the first they had seen in many months. However, it didn't provide them with any blubber.

Once the blubber was gone—and it was very low—they would have to eat their seal and penguin raw. True, they still had a few of the dogs. They had been saving these on the faint hope that it might yet be possible to get back to Ocean Camp. On March 29th a big segment of the floe split off, and once again, for an instant, they thought they were goners. However, this break was a break indeed, for it revealed a sea leopard, peeking over the edge. The man it peered at was a short one—and a quick thinker. He flapped his arms, imitating a penguin, while Frank Wild dived for his rifle.

The sea leopard is a large, vicious beast, a kind of seal that operates alone, never in packs. It is voracious, very voracious. It often wriggles out of the water to gulp a stray penguin or two. This one never did get its "penguin." Wild's rifle spoke, and the creature collapsed.

It was all of 11 feet long, and yielded almost 1,000 pounds of meat, besides at least a two weeks' supply of lovely, lovely blubber. There was an additional prize. In the stomach were almost fifty undigested fish. These were put aside for future use.

The next day they killed the balance of the dogs and ate them. To their amazement the meat was not tough but tasty and tender. It was much like veal.

There were birds overhead, for the first time, and that was encouraging. It started to rain, and that wasn't. The floe was melting.

They had floated past Paulet, their first goal, and on April 6th they sighted Clarence, one of the two remote islands, the other being Elephant.

Early on the morning of April 8th, the floe cracked wide open, and suddenly there was water all around, and the men ran for the boats.

CHAPTER 22

DESPITE the drills, the take-off was a disorderly one. They were over-anxious. The gear was not properly stowed, so that movement was awkward and hampered. No provision had been made for a man at each bow with an extra oar to stave off small floes. It was difficult for the boats to keep close without bumping. The raised sides made rowing almost impossible, and even when the thwarts upon which the rowers sat were also raised by means of packing cases, the position was an unnatural one. Moreover, the men were all soft from lack of exercise.

The world around them still was flat, and there was no landmark, nothing to steer by. Nor was navigation easy. In that latitude at that time of the year, approaching the southern winter, 16 or 17 hours out of every 24 were dark or at least dim, and the sun was seldom visible even in the short stretch of daylight.

Nevertheless, in a matter of minutes they had left behind them that rotting platter of ice that had been their home for many months. They could not have found it again if they had wished—and they did not wish to.

In many ways they might have thought their new quarters more secure than Camp Patience had been, if at least equally uncomfortable, for these were not run-of-the-mill lifeboats to which they had entrusted themselves.

The leader, *James Caird,* was a whale boat, double-ended, 22 feet six inches in length, six feet three inches at her greatest beam. She mounted two masts and could spread a mainsail, a jib, and a small mizzen far aft. Made of Baltic pine, American elm, and British oak, she was the lightest of the three, by a little the largest, and by a great deal the fastest. She now carried 11 men, including Ernest Henry Shackleton, who was in charge.

The other two were Norwegian-built cutters, square-sterned, made of solid oak, 21 feet nine inches overall, six feet two inches in the beam. Each carried one stubby mast, but the *Dudley Docker* had a fore-and-aft rig, whereas the *Stancomb-Wills* had only a lug sail and so could not be taken into the wind. The *Docker* carried nine men, with Worsley in charge, who did all the navigating. The *Stancomb-Wills* carried eight men, with Hudson in charge. They were strong boats, yes, but they were open, undecked, and—if they ever got away from that damned ice—about to enter the most turbulent, most treacherous sea in the world.

The men were scarcely fragrant. They had not washed in half a year, and many, even most, still

155

had diarrhea. Overhead, the birds, which, intent on fish, had ignored the floe, now hung low and thick, and they didn't care where they defecated, splattering the occupants of the three gallant boats. As soon as they reached open water and the going got rough, some of the men became seasick, and the sour smell of vomit was added to all the others.

The first night they slept on a floe, which cracked open, dropping one of the men, sleeping bag and all, into the sea. Shackleton was there instantly—he had been prowling the camp, worrying—and he hauled the man out seconds before the crack snapped shut.

The victim was one of the two firemen, Ernest Holness. He wasn't too scared—it had all happened so swiftly—but he was miffed at having lost his tobacco. There was no dry clothing, and the men worked in relays all night, walking him around and around the floe to keep him alive. It was bitter cold, and a killing wind came whistling up from the south, all the way from the Pole. The water froze on Holness, so that he clinked as he walked.

The next night, unable to find a suitable floe, they slept in the hove-to empty boats—when they slept at all. The thermometers had been packed away, so they could not tell the temperature, but it was certainly well below zero. All around them, throughout that fearsome night, killer whales were surfacing, spouting steam, submerging again. They were huge beasts, and there was always a chance that one of them would come up under the boats.

On April 12th they came out at last into the open sea, but it was blowing such a gale they had to take refuge up a water lead, back among the protective ice, and they spent that night on a rotten berg-floe that threatened to break up at any moment. It was here that the *other* fireman, William Stevenson, fell into the sea and had to be hauled out and walked about. He, however, retained his 'baccy.

While still in the pack, they had drifted past Paulet. Now, again in the open, they were making a course for tiny remote King George Island, where there would be some chance of being visited by a whaler, but when after many hours of painful pulling the sun came out for a little while and Worsley hastened to make a calculation, they learned—and it was a horrible blow—that in spite of southeast wind they had been making a lot of east longitude, thanks to an unseen but powerful current. They were now actually farther away from any land than they had been at Patience Camp.

They changed course, making for Hope Bay at the very tip of the Antarctic Peninsula, which should have been about 130 miles away.

It was snowing, and the seas were mountainous.

They were blown off their course once again and forced to make for either Clarence or Elephant, the two southernmost of the South Falkland Islands, about 100 miles to the northwest.

They had had only a few hours' sleep in the past four days and nights, and the wonder was that none of them had died of sheer exhaustion. One, Rickinson, did suffer a heart attack, brought about by his exertions.

Water kept flooding the boats, and they had to bail all the time. They were soaked through.

They had to row all the time too, or the boats would have been swamped. The wind was too high to permit any spread of canvas. A sea-anchor was tried, and it jerked them back and forth, but it was made of half-decayed tents and not strong enough to hold all three boats in line.

Within less than a mile of Elephant Island, they were smashed by a williwaw, a sudden, stupendous burst of wind that crashed down from the hills upon the nearby water, the dread of all round-the-Horners since Drake.

Caird and *Stancomb-Wills* managed to stay together, but the *Docker* with Worsley and the navigating instruments, were lost—it seemed.

The *Stancomb-Wills* and *Caird,* badly battered but still somehow afloat, staggered into a bay of Elephant Island with the sickly light of dawn, and there, while they were catching their collective breath and preparing to run aground on a piece of land never before touched by the foot of man, the *Dudley Docker* quietly joined them.

Sir Ernest had promised the steward-stowaway, Percy Blackboro, that because of the hardihood he had shown he would be granted the privilege of being the first to step ashore on this barren beach. But this was not to be. Young Blackboro was too stiff to move, and they had to carry him ashore. Even then, he could not stand erect, for his feet were frostbitten.

The others toddled drunkenly about, picking up stones, stamping, patting one another on the shoulders, or sitting down, swaying back and forth, muttering gibberish. They could hardly believe it. Here was the first time that they had been on land in almost a year and a half.

After a while they ate enormously, pulled the boats up a little farther, and fell to the ground and went to sleep. It was still snowing.

This was land, all right, but it was no Garden of Eden. It was located at 61 degrees five minutes south, 55 degrees ten minutes West, and it was about 23 miles long, east-west, and 13 miles across at its widest point, a solid mass of disagreeableness. There were no trees, only bare, jagged rocks, some of them 2,500-foot peaks. A rookery of ringed (chinstrap) penguins, near the place where they had landed, looked promising at first, but they departed the next day. There were a few Gentoos—a grubbier, tougher penguin—from time to time, and skuas, and Cape gulls. The sea elephant, the species of seal from which the island got its name, was plentiful. There were lichens and even some seaweed, if you looked hard enough.

In the morning Shackleton saw that this scrawny beach upon which they found themselves would never do as a camp site, for there were evidences that the tide from time to time washed it out entirely. He sent Wild in one of the boats to explore the coast to the west, while he and Hurley did the same to the east, on foot. They located nothing suitable, but Wild was soon back with news of a rocky spit of land not far to the west that should serve their purposes. They called this Point Wild, and they moved there—in a raging blizzard.

All of the tents were worn and patched, and Tent 5 some time ago had been blown completely away, so that now Shackleton gave members of that tent crew permission to take the mast out of the *Docker,* haul her well up on the spit, and overturn her, and sleep underneath. The other tents would not last long in that wind; there was no protection from it. It banged down from the cliffs, even on the lee side of the island. The men tried to dig a cave out of the side of a hill, but the ground was fast-frozen. They tried to construct a stone hut, but the stones, worn by the weather, were uniformly round, and they had nothing that could conceivably be used as cement. At last they dismasted the *Stancomb-Wills* and turned her upside down beside the *Docker*, and with these two as a roof they built a habitation of sorts with stones and mud and snow and sleazy old blankets.

All of this time the blizzard raged. It got even worse.

All of this time too, McNeish, assisted by McLeod and Marston, was strengthening the *James Caird*, for the Boss meant to take this cockleshell to South Georgia, 800 miles away, as soon as the weather permitted.

160

Why not? Somebody had to go and get help. The men might survive a winter on this highly inhospitable island, but with the coming of spring in September, they still could not reasonably hope to be spotted and rescued by some stray whaler. So they would have to go and get their own help; and the person to do that, obviously, was Ernest Henry Shackleton. They were his boys, weren't they?

CHAPTER 23

HE MADE formal announcement of the fact, but he might have saved himself the trouble, for it had been an open secret ever since they came to Cape Wild, if for no other reason than that everybody could see what McNeish, McLeod, and Marston were doing to the "flagship."

The sides of the *Caird* already had been raised, so that she had a depth of seven feet five inches. Most of this was now decked over, leaving an open hatch about four feet by two aft, for the tillerman. As a framework, they used two runners taken from a discarded sledge back at Patience Camp, and they planked these over with boards taken from the raised sides of the *Dudley Docker*. These boards in turn were covered with tight-stretched canvas. The mast from the *Docker* was fastened along the bottom of the *Caird,* inside, in order to strengthen the keel. A ton of rocks was then stowed below as ballast. Of rocks, on Elephant, they had plenty. All this work, except the ballasting, was done while the blizzard raged.

Always a competent carpenter, McNeish might

have been expected to take particular pains with the strengthening of the *Caird,* for he was to be one of the crew. The choice, just at first, might seem a strange one. The disapproving, puritanical McNeish was hardly a jolly companion in close quarters, and Shackleton had never forgiven him for what he had viewed as disloyalty. Yet, if you have to have a troublemaker, it is as well to keep him within sight, within reach. The 22 men to be left behind, under Frank Wild, would have a bad enough time of it in their 18-by-ten-by-five-foot shack without being made to put up with the services of a sea lawyer.

Also, it was possible that the *Caird* might get banged about a bit by ice floes, in which case McNeish's services would be in demand, whereas there was nothing more that he could do, along carpentry lines, on the island.

Another of the non-officers chosen—practically everybody in the expedition had volunteered—was John Vincent, who at one time had threatened to be a troublemaker himself. Back aboard the *Endurance,* Vincent, by sheer strength and bullying tactics, had made himself the unofficial bosun, the king of the forecastle, until a few of the others had quietly protested to Shackleton. The Boss then had had a long talk with John Vincent, and there was no more fuss.

The third non-officer was Timothy McCarty, sinewy, able, willing, rugged, unfailingly good-natured.

Tom Crean, too, was rugged, a man who would take no nonsense from anybody.

Worsley would navigate. He had his own sextant and also one borrowed from Hudson, and he had the only chronometer left; the others had gone down with the *Endurance*. He would need to be very good to hit so tiny an island after 800 miles of wild sea and only an occasional peek at the sun. Tierra del Fuego or the South Falklands, both more or less due north, were nearer to Elephant—one 500 miles, the other 550 miles, but to try for either would mean to buck the prevailing winds.

They were strong men, all six of them. They were muscular. They'd need to be.

They took a six weeks' supply of food, most of it sledging rations intended for a different sort of dash—the dash to the South Pole—and two Primus stoves, a homemade pump, six reindeer sleeping bags, two 18-gallon casks full of melted ice from a nearby glacier. The water was not entirely free of salt, some of which must have got on the surface of the glacier in the form of sea spume; but Shackleton, who tasted it, said that it would do.

The snow stopped and the wind fell the morning of April 24th. The blizzard was over. The sun even came out for a little while, an event of which Worsley took prompt advantage. He knew their location from charts, but he wished to check the accuracy of their only remaining chronometer. This turned out to be good.

From a high place on the island they spotted a rift among the ice floes, a rift easily big enough to admit the *Caird*. Then, after a certain amount of handshaking and somewhat forced raillery, cracks about bed linen and *pâté de fois gras* and all that, they pushed off, all three sails set.

For a couple of days they had it fairly easy, though getting through the ice pack was a trickier business than it had looked from afar. Some of the berg-floes were so big they blocked the wind from the sails, and the *Caird* had to be rowed, an awkward stunt from a flush deck.

Instead of going straight northeast-by-east, it was Shackleton's plan to go due north for a while, then bear about and go due east the rest of the way. This would mean they would cover far more than the 800 miles that extend between Elephant and South Georgia, but at the same time it would have certain distinct advantages. It would get them north of the ice pack sooner than a direct northeast-by-east course, and this was important, particularly at night, when they could be smashed to smithereens without a moment's notice. Also, it would mean that when they emerged into the dreaded Drake's Passage, the seas would be sweeping in behind them, from west to east, instead of at an oblique angle, which would be perilous for so small a boat.

The third day the wind unexpectedly shifted to due north, and since they had not yet reached the parallel of latitude they needed, they had no choice but to buck it, tacking, getting just about nowhere. This, however, did not last long.

They were uncomfortable enough, in all conscience, even when riding before the wind. The *Caird* took on a great deal of green water, besides the spray, which was especially thick at the smothered tops of the Cape Horn rollers, called "graybeards" by mariners who had seen waves estimated to exceed a mile in length from crest to crest and 60 feet in height. She was cranky in the bows and would dip under, to come up with a jolting jerk that was hard on everybody but in particular on the members of the off-watch who were trying to sleep up there. She had never done this before, and Worsley suggested that she might be over-ballasted. Two thousand pounds was a lot. Why didn't they throw out some of the rocks? Shackleton said no, for the sensible reason that once thrown overboard those rocks could not be recovered. What if it turned out that she was *under*-ballasted?

The water would find its way down the open hold or through cracks in the deck canvas, so that everything below was wet, sleeping bags included, and they had to pump four or five times a day. At night sometimes the spray froze, and one of the men had to go about with a hand axe, chopping the ice away, lest the craft capsize. This was an exceedingly risky business on that bucking bronco of a boat.

Their own water was not very good. It had more salt in it than Shackleton had supposed. One of the casks had fallen overboard while they were loading supplies, and some sea water must have seeped in. Their thirst was terrible, almost as terrible as their suffering from the cold, nor were they granted any rain.

More than once Shackleton, gripping the tiller, must have quoted grimly through clenched teeth, if that was possible, a familiar stanza from his beloved Coleridge:

> *Water, water, everywhere,*
> *And all the boards did shrink;*
> *Water, water, everywhere*
> *Nor any drop to drink.*

On May 6th there was a touch of sun, the only touch they ever did have, and Worsley got busy and announced that they were about 100 miles from the northwest corner of South Georgia, which should lie dead ahead.

Sure enough, two days later they sighted land. That would be the high white peaks behind King Haakon Bay, on the other side of the island from Stromness Bay, where the little whaling station of Grytviken was located, the last bit of civilization they had seen a year and a half ago.

They meant to go to Grytviken, but the elements intervened. It was like the approach to Elephant Island all over again. It was as though Nature was playing a little game of cat-and-mouse with them. Just a few miles from the coast, when everything seemed to be going fine, they were hit by a gale that soon blew up to hurricane proportions. They lost their rudder and would have lost their mainmast had they not been driven, willy-nilly, just in time, into the protection of a subsidiary of King Haakon Bay. Out of control, they drove into a cove, where luckily there was a stream of fresh water. And thus ended what many historians consider the most extraordinary small boat voyage ever made. (See Appendix B.)

They rested, uneasily, until the storm blew over. Then they made their way to another part of the bay, and pulled the boat up and overturned it, making a shelter. They called this Peggoty Camp.

Vincent and McNeish were in very poor shape, not able to go on. The rest, though shaken, were all right. To try to sail around to Stromness Bay, with the boat in the condition it was and two men virtually sleeping-bag-ridden, was unthinkable. To walk around the shore, some 150 miles, even if it was possible, would take too long. Shackleton decreed that he and Crean and Worsley would strike straight out across the island. McCarty would be left to take care of McNeish and Vincent.

Another dash.

They started very early on the morning of May 19th, carrying with them some Bovril, some biscuits, a carpenter's axe for cutting ice, 50 feet of Alpine rope, and a box containing 48 matches.

They got off to a good, brisk start, and by dawn they reckoned that they were about 3,000 feet up. They were overlooking a large bay.

There were no maps of the interior of South Georgia. Nobody had ever gone there. Why should anybody? There was only one settlement, the whaling station at the northeast corner of the island. They knew that whaling station well, having spent almost a month there.

However, the *coast* had been charted, if in a sketchy sort of way, and they had a copy of that map. From it they gathered that the body of water they were looking down upon was Possession Bay. Between them and the northeastern corner of the island there were only mountains—lovely, snow-covered ranges—and glaciers. There might be other mountains and other glaciers beyond those. They would go and have a look.

They picked what seemed to be a gap and made for it. They reached it at eleven o'clock in the morning and found themselves faced with a sheer rock drop. They had their homemade Alpine shoes, spiked with screws. They had their rope, their ice axe, and, God knows, they had plenty of courage; but the gap was impassable. There was nothing for them to do but turn back.

They found another gap, and examined this and it was the same story all over again. They made for a third.

In a sheltered spot they rested for a little while with their backs to a rock. Shackleton allowed them to sleep for five minutes, then awakened them and told them that they had slept for half an hour. They struggled on.

The way now, in search of a third gap, a passable one, was over a glacier, and in the early part of the night the moon shone brightly, which was well, for there were many crevasses. At last they came to a steep falloff—ice this time, not rock. There could be no more turning back. They were

169

on a very high place, with no protection from the wind, and without sleeping bags or blankets. If they stayed there for any length of time, if they were overtaken by sleep or numbness, they would freeze to death. Shackleton climbed over the edge.

The moon had gone down, and they could hear Shackleton hacking out steps with McNeish's adze, though they could not see him. He stopped and called to them to come down.

He was on a ledge, and the descent beyond that point—or what little they could see of it— was not so steep, though in truth it was steep enough. If they had to hack out toeholds the whole distance down—however far that was— they probably would not survive the night. But they must keep moving, somehow. There were the three men on King Haakon Bay to think of, and the 22 men on Elephant. Shackleton announced that they would slide down on the seats of their pants.

It looked like madness, but they were desperate. They might end up in a crevasse, or smash against an outjutting of rock, or be swept right off the edge of a cliff. It was a chance they would have to take.

Shackleton coiled the rope into three flat plates, one behind the other, and he sat down on the first of these. Worsley sat on the second, holding the Boss's shoulders, and Crean sat on the third, holding Worsley's shoulders. They were for all the world like three bobsledders without a sled. They pushed off.

They could see nothing. Blackness and cold air *whooshed* past them. It might have taken two minutes, it might have taken as much as three, before they found themselves pitched into a snowdrift.

They rose, brushing themselves off, and shook hands all around, congratulating one another on still being alive. It had been a miracle. They estimated that they had slid for about a mile, and that they were now almost 3,000 feet lower than they had been when at the top of the glacier. They made themselves a little hoosh, tightened up, and pushed on.

Dawn of the second day found them looking out over what must have been Husvik Harbor, only about twelve miles from Grytviken. Those twelve miles would not be easy strolling—at one point they had to lower themselves by means of the rope, one by one, through a waterfall. But they were to be as a rose-lined garden path compared with what lay behind them.

At seven o'clock, within sight of the whaling station, they heard a steam whistle, calling all hands to the factory. It was the sweetest sound they had ever listened to.

At a little after one o'clock in the afternoon, or just about 36 hours from the time they had started from Camp Peggoty, they tottered into Grytviken.

The first to see them, two small boys, ran away, screaming.

They paused to ask an old man the way to the factory, but he couldn't answer, for he was gaping in fright at these subhuman-looking creatures.

What were they? Where had they come from? They went toward the factory, these ragged, shuffling, sagging, stinking, red-eyed men with their matted hair and beards. The manager came out. He had known them all, and well, but he did not know them now.

"Who in hell *are* you?" he cried.

The scarecrow in the middle stepped forward apologetically.

"My name is Shackleton," he said in a quiet voice.

The manager burst into tears.

CHAPTER 24

THE ICE WAS THICK that winter in the Weddell Sea. Shackleton sailed in the *Southern Sky* relief ship from Grytviken May 23rd, but three days later, when they reached the ice—a good 70 miles from Elephant Island—they could find no lead through it. Being coaled for only ten days, they could not spend much time looking, and they turned to Port Stanley in the Falklands, which they reached May 31st. From there Shackleton sent a long letter to his wife and wireless messages to the Admiralty and to the Royal Society. It was the first the world knew that he was alive. June 10th he sailed from Port Stanley in the trawler *Instituto de Pesca No. 1,* lent to him by the government of Uruguay, but despite a prolonged and gallant try, they could not reach Elephant. Fog was the reason this time. They could not even glimpse the island. By the same token, Shackleton reflected on the way back to Port Stanley, the 22 men on the island would not have been able to see *them,* and hence would not be overwhelmed by disappointment when the trawler turned away.

He went by mailboat to Punta Arenas, Chile, where a group of British businessmen raised money for him to charter the wooden schooner *Emma,* and the Chilean government lent the steamer *Yelcho* as a tow boat, on the understanding that the *Yelcho,* which was of steel construction, would not be exposed to the ice pack. Both vessels, after bucking a high southern gale for two days, were forced to turn back on July 14th.

He knew a relief vessel was being fitted out in England, but he did not think that he should wait for this. He was advised to relax until the weather did, but he could never do so while his men suffered. He persuaded the Chilean government to lend him the *Yelcho* once more, and this time she towed the *Emma* near enough to Elephant Island so that the schooner could move in under her own steam—for she carried an auxiliary engine. This was August 30th, 1916.

Standing in the bow of a gig, Ernest Henry Shackleton started for shore. He could see the tiny dark, figures waiting for him, and he counted and recounted them anxiously. Yes. Twenty-two.

As soon as he got near enough to make it practical, he put his hands to his mouth.

"Are you all right?" he shouted.

On the shore, Frank Wild grinned. They all grinned at least a little. "All right" had a strange sound, in the circumstances. But it was answerable. After all, they *were.* They were alive, which was a great deal. No need to bother Sir Ernest with the painful details right now. Why mention the tooth that Kerr had had to have pulled, or

Hudson's stubborn abscess, or Greenstreet's frost-bitten feet, or Wordie's infected hand, or Rickinson's boils? Why relate, here, the story of how Drs. Macklin and McIlroy had to amputate all the toes of young Blackboro's left foot, in order to forestall gangrene? Or even mention, just now, Greenstreet's imperishable diary entry, "So passes another goddam rotten day," which could have applied to them all during these past four months? That could come later.

Frank Wild saluted in the direction of the racing gig.

"All present and accounted for, Boss," he cried.

THE END

APPENDIX A

SHOVING ASIDE the vague, time-hazed, and unverifiable reports of ancient Dutch, Spanish, and Portuguese navigators who spied some huge landmass to the south when blown off course, or thought that they did, the honor of "discovering" the continent of Antarctica—that is, of first seeing it, for none of them made any attempt to land there—is disputed by the adherents of three men.

The first is Bellinghausen. The Soviet Union has lately seen fit to put forth his claims on the basis of his fully published journal, and to contend that he first saw Antarctica near the 41st meridian of east longitude, early in 1820. He certainly saw something. It might have been part of Enderby Land or it might have been some bergs. Atmospheric conditions being what they were, it was impossible to be sure. Granted, many birds were sighted, which made it look like land instead of simply ice, but Bellinghausen, a very careful man, saw no proof that it was in fact land, and he wrote it down as ice. Present-day Russians insist that he made a mistake.

On the other side of the continent is its northernmost point, the only part that extends any considerable distance above the Antarctic Circle and hence the most likely to be seen first. This is an enormous peninsula. When fully charted, it will probably prove to be the biggest peninsula in the world. It pointed north almost directly at South America, with which, it seems probable, Antarctica was at one time geographically connected, being a continuation of the Andes chain. Both Chile and Argentina claim this peninsula, and so does Great Britain.

A few days after Bellinghausen might or might not have sighted the continent thousands of miles away, Captain Edward Bransfield, Royal Navy, who was deliberately looking for it, might or might not have sighted part of the peninsula. A little earlier than either of them, Nathaniel Brown Palmer of Stonington, Connecticut may or may not have spotted the mainland from a high place on a nearby island. Palmer, 21 years old at the time, was looking for new sealing grounds in the tiny *Hero* with a crew of five. He assuredly saw and to some extent explored the coast of this peninsula several months later, as the log of the *Hero* in the Library of Congress shows.

The British, insisting that Bransfield was the real discoverer, had officially given the peninsula the name he gave it, Graham Land, in honor of Sir James R. G. Graham, first Lord of the Admiralty in his day. The Americans, declaring that what Bransfield saw was only Trinity Island off the coast, and that Palmer had glimpsed the mainland first anyway, had called the peninsula, officially, Palmer Land.

To make the matter even more complicated, Argentina calls it San Martin Land; Chile calls it O'Higgins Land.

The Palmer-Bransfield dispute generated a great deal of geographic heat on both sides of the Atlantic, including some highly unprofessorial accusations, so that at the time of the International Geophysical Year of 1957-58, the consultants tactfully agreed to call the place, for working purposes, the Antarctic Peninsula. Later, American, British, Australian, and New Zealand mapmakers decided to bury the hatchet by calling it Antarctic Peninsula, officially and permanently. The northern part would be called Graham Land; the southern part Palmer Land, and Palmer Archipelago—a group of islands off that coast—would keep its name. This agreement finally became official when it was approved by the United States Board on Geographic Names, an agency of the Department of the Interior, and the report was endorsed by Secretary Stewart L. Udall.

APPENDIX B

IT WOULD be absurd to say that the distressed men on one small boat trip of emergency had a better or worse time than those on another. There is no sense in comparing them. The voyage of the *James Caird* broke no records of length, time, men involved, or lack of supplies, but it was surely one of the grimmest in history in regard to the seas encountered, the winds, and the ice.

The 3,618 nautical-mile voyage of the *Bounty's* 23-foot launch, with 19 men aboard, from Tofoa in the Friendly Islands (now Tonga) to Timor in the Dutch East Indies is of course a classic. That was in April and May of 1789 after the famous mutiny. The trip took 44 days, but not all of these were spent at sea, for they made several stopovers. They were given by the mutineers 150 pounds of bread, 32 pounds of pork, six quarts of rum, six bottles of wine, and 28 gallons of water, but they were able to replenish this with oysters, coconuts, and breadfruit, besides fresh water, at the various islands they touched, and even at sea they caught an occasional fish, and an occasional fowl. It must be remembered, too, that these were tropical waters and the men met with few storms, and no big ones.

November 20, 1821, in the Pacific, three of the four whaleboats of the *Essex of Nantucket* put out to harpoon whales. One of the boats was badly damaged by a tail-swipe and turned back to the ship. The ship itself was then attacked head-on by an infuriated 85-foot sperm whale, which charged it twice at great speed and made two gaping hull holes. The ship started to sink. In a matter of minutes the men aboard got the fourth boat launched under command of the mate, Owen Chase. The other two boats returning from the chase with the captain and nineteen crewmen, got what little supplies they could off the *Essex of Nantucket*—600 pounds of bread and 65 gallons of water—before she sank utterly. Then they started for the mainland, more than 1,000 miles away. They had navigating instruments, and they made it, though their sufferings from hunger and thirst were acute. The incident is notable because it gave Herman Melville the idea for *Moby Dick*. He undoubtedly read Chase's thrilling firsthand report.

Dr. Elisha Kane, a Philadelphia physician, had 15 men in his command when in the Spring of 1855 he found himself hopelessly icebound at the tiny Eskimo community of Etah, Greenland. They had been out looking for the lost Sir John Franklin Arctic expedition, and they were 1,300 miles from the nearest Danish settlement. They had three boats, *Faith, Hope,* and—no, not *Charity—Red Eric*. This last was the smallest and weakest, and it was used as a supply boat at first and later abandoned altogether. The other two were double-ended whaleboats, undecked, 26 feet long, three feet deep, with seven feet of beam. Dr. Kane, like Shackleton, was a natural leader, and he brought them all back alive. It took from May 18th to August 1st.

World War II broke many records, including some of those pertaining to small boat voyages. Perhaps the most notable was that of the jolly boat of the British freighter *Anglo-Saxon*, which was sunk by a surface raider off the west coast of Africa on September 13th, 1940. The jolly boat, an 18-footer, with seven men aboard, including the first mate and the radio operator, was the only thing that floated free from that wreck. Five of those men died within the first 24 days, going west. They had no navigation instruments, though they did have four oars and a lug sail. The two remaining seamen stuck it out, on a starvation diet, until they found themselves beached at Eluthera in the Bahamas, more than 3,000 miles away from the scene of the attack. It had taken them 71 days, during which time they had sighted no sail and, of course, no land. They kept track of those days by cutting notches into the gunnel of the jolly boat. You can still see those notches, for the boat is preserved at the Mystic Seaport, Mystic, Connecticut.

The *James Caird*, too, was saved for posterity. It is open to public view at Dulwich College, London, England.

AUTHORITIES

ANTARCTIC EXPLORERS, like the first missionaries to what was at the time called the Sandwich Islands (Hawaii), for the most part were impressed by the historic significance of their job, and almost all of them kept diaries, and kept them conscientiously. They were a highly literate lot.

The real work of preparing this book, then, was not in getting material, of which there is plenty; the real work was in winnowing out from that huge mass of facts what seemed pertinent and colorful and significant, and in checking subsequent accounts with on-the-spot accounts and descriptions. Besides the books listed below, the files of *The New York Times* and the London *Times* were used extensively, and the writer wishes to thank the dedicated reference librarians at the Mystic Seaport, Mystic, Connecticut; the Yale University Library; the Phoebe Griffin Noyes Library, Old Lyme, Connecticut; the Olin Memorial Library, Wesleyan University; and the Palmer Library, Connecticut College for Women.

Armitage, Albert B., *Two Years in the Antarctic, Being a Narrative of the British National Antarctic Expedition.* London; Edward Arnold, 1905.

Amundsen, Roald, *The South Pole: Norwegian Antarctic Expedition in the "Fram", 1910-12.* London, John Murray, 1912 (Two volumes).

Bagshawe, Thomas Wyatt, *Two Men in the Antarctic.* Cambridge, Cambridge University Press, 1939.

Balch, Edwin Swift, *Antarctica.* Philadelphia, Allen, Lane & Scott, 1902.

Begbie, Harold, *Shackleton: A Memory.* London, Mills & Boon, 1922.

Bellinghausen, Fabian Gottleib Von, *The Voyage of Captain Bellinghausen to the Antarctic Seas, 1819-21,* Translated from the Russian by Frank Debenham. London, The Hakluyt Society, 1945 (Two volumes).

Bennett, A. G., *Whaling in the Antarctic.* Edinburgh, W. Blackwood & Sons, 1931.

Bernacchi, Louis, *To the South Polar Regions: Expedition of 1898-1900.* London, Hurst and Blackett, Ltd., 1901.

Borchgrevink, C. E., *First on the Antarctic Continent, Being an Account of the British Antarctic Expedition, 1898-1900.* London, G. Newnes, 1901.

Bruce, W. S., *Polar Exploration.* London, Williams & Norgate, 1911.

Burney, J., *History of the Discoveries in the South Sea or Pacific Ocean.* London, 1803-17 (Five volumes).

Byrd, Richard Evelyn. *Discovery, The Story of the Second Byrd Expedition*. New York, G. P. Putnam's Sons, 1935.

Byrd, Richard Evelyn, *Little America: Aerial Exploration in the Antarctic*. New York, G. P. Putnam's Sons, 1930.

Caras, Robert A., *Antarctica: Land of Frozen Time*. Philadelphia, Chilton Books, 1962.

Charcot, Dr. Jean, *The Voyage of the "Why Not?" in the Antarctic: The Journal of the Second French South Polar Expedition, 1908-1910*, Translated by Philip Walsh. London, Hodder & Stoughton, 1911.

Cherry-Garrard, Apsley, *The Worst Journey in the World*. London, Constable & Company, Ltd., 1922.

Christie, E. Wm. H., *The Antarctic Problem: An Historical and Political Study*. London, Allen & Unwin, 1951.

Daly, Reginald A., *The Changing World of the Ice Age*. New Haven, Yale University Press, 1934.

Debenham, Frank, *Discovery and Exploration*. New York, Doubleday & Company, 1960.

Debenham, Frank, *See* Bellinghausen.

Delano, Amasa, *Narrative of Voyages and Travels in the Northern Hemispheres*. Boston, E. G. House, 1817.

Dufek, George John, *Operation Deep Freeze*. New York, Harcourt, Brace & World, 1957.

Fanning, Edmund, *Voyages Around the World*. New York, Collins & Hannay, 1833.

Fisher, Margery and James, *Shackleton*. London, James Barrie Books, Ltd., 1957.

Frazier, Paul W., *Antarctic Assault*. New York, Dodd, Mead & Co., 1959.

Fricker, Karl, *The Antarctic Regions*. New York, The Macmillan Company, 1904.

Goebel, Julius, *The Struggle for the Falkland Islands: A Study in Legal and Diplomatic History*. New Haven, Yale University Press, 1927.

Gould, Laurence M., *Antarctica in World Affairs*. New York, Foreign Policy Association, 1958.

Greely, Adolphus Washington, *The Polar Regions in the Twentieth Century: Their Discovery and Industrial Evolution*. Boston, Little, Brown and Co., 1928.

Greely, Adolphus Washington, *Three Years of Arctic Service*. New York, Charles Scribner's Sons, 1886.

Hayes, J. Gordon, *Antarctica: A Treatise on the South Continent*. London, The Richards Press, Ltd., 1928.

Hayes, J. Gordon, *The Conquest of the South Pole: Antarctic Exploration, 1906 to 1930*. London, T. Butterworth, 1932.

Hayward, Walter B., *The Last Continent of Adventure*. New York, Dodd, Mead & Company, 1930.

Henry, Thomas R., *The White Continent: the Story of Antarctica*. New York, William Sloan Associates, 1950.

Herman, Paul, *The Great Age of Discovery*. New York, Harper & Row, 1958.

Hobbs, William Herbert, *Explorers of the Antarctic*. New York, House of Field, Inc., 1941.

Hurley, Frank, *Argonauts of the South*. New York, G. P. Putnam's Sons, 1925.

Hussey, Dr. L. D. A., *South with Shackleton*. London, Sampson Low, 1951.

Joerg, W. L. G., *Brief History of Polar Exploration Since the Introduction of Flying*. New York, American Geographical Society, 1930.

Joerg, W. L. G., editor, *Problems of Polar Research, A series of papers by thirty-one authors*. New York, American Geographical Society, 1928.

Jones, Stephen B., *The Arctic: Problems and Possibilities*. New Haven, Yale Institute of International Studies, 1948.

Kearns, William H., Jr., and Britton, Beverley, *The Silent Continent*. New York, Harper & Row, 1955.

Lansing, Alfred, *Endurance: Shackleton's Incredible Voyage*. New York, McGraw-Hill Book Company, Inc., 1959.

MacCormick, R., *Voyages of Discovery in the Arctic and Antarctic Seas and Round the World*. London, Simpson Low, Marston, Searle, and Rivington, 1884.

Markham, Sir Clements R., *The Lands of Silence: A History of Arctic and Antarctic Exploration*. Cambridge, Cambridge University Press, 1921.

Mathews, Mary Alice, *The Arctic and Antarctic Regions, With Special Reference to Territorial Claims*. Washington, Carnegie Endowment for International Peace, 1940.

Mill, Hugh Robert, *The Siege of the South Pole: The Story of Antarctic Exploration*. London, Alston Rivers, 1905.

Mirsky, Jeannette, *To the North! The Story of Arctic Exploration from Earliest Times to the Present*. New York, The Viking Press, 1934.

Mitterling, Philip I., *America in the Antarctic to 1840*. Urbana, University of Illinois Press, 1959.

Owen, Russell, *The Antarctic Ocean*. New York, McGraw-Hill, 1941.

Scott, Robert Falcon, *Scott's Last Expedition*. London, Smith, Elder & Company, 1913 (Two volumes).

Shackleton, Ernest Henry, *South!* New York, The Macmillan Company, 1926.

Shackleton, Ernest Henry, *The Heart of the Antarctic*. London, Heinemann, 1909 (Two volumes).

Stackpole, Edouard A., *The Voyage of the Huron and the Huntress; The American Sealers and the Discovery of the Continent of Antarctica*. Mystic, Conn., The Marine Historical Association, Inc., 1955.

Stackpole, Edouard A., *The Sea-Hunters: The Great Age of Whaling*. Philadelphia, J. B. Lippincott Company, 1953.

Sullivan, Walter, *Quest for a Continent*. New York, McGraw-Hill, 1957.

187

Taylor, T. Griffith, *Antarctic Adventure and Research*. London, D. Appleton, 1930.

Weems, John Edward, *Race for the Pole*. New York, Henry Holt & Co., 1960.

Wild, Frank, *Shackleton's Last Voyage: the Story of the Quest*. London, Cassell, 1923.

Williamson, James A., *Cook and the Opening of the Pacific*. New York, The Macmillan Company, 1948.

Worsley, Frank A., *Endurance, an Epic of Polar Adventure*. London, Philip Allen & Co., Ltd., 1931.

Worsley, Frank A., *Shackleton's Boat Journey*. London, Philip Allen & Co., Ltd., 1933.

A POLAR GLOSSARY

Aurora australis A luminous atmospheric phenomenon resembling a shimmering
curtain of irridescent lights. Elec-
trical in origin, it is the Antarctic equivalent of the northern
lights.

Aurora borealis The northern lights; visible in
the Northern Hemisphere.

Bergschrund A crevasse or series of crevasses
at the entrance to a glacier.

Bergy bit A bit of floating ice less than 30
feet across and perhaps 15 feet
high above the water; a small
iceberg.

Brash Mushy floating ice, consisting of
ground-up floes and lumps of
snow.

Calve	Process of cleavage whereby a large chunk of ice breaks off an iceberg.
Crevasse	A crack or fissure in a glacier.
Fata Morgana	An optical illusion or mirage; a trick of light.
Finnskoes	(Norwegian for "Finns' shoes") A large overshoe made of reindeer hide and used at once as a sort of snowshoe.
Floe	A flat piece of floating ice.
Frazil ice	Ice just beginning to form on the surface of the water. Also called "lolly ice."
Gorgie	(Combination of gorge and orgy.) A feast far from home; an unrationed meal or treat.
Hoosh	A thick heavy soup made out of just about anything that is handy; a sledging meal.
Ice blink	An Antarctic light phenomenon by means of which near or distant objects seem to disappear, reappear, in the hazy deceptive half-light before winter sets in.

Névé	Crystalline or granulated snow on the top of a glacier snow that has not yet been compressed into ice.
Pemmican	A cake made of meat paste, flavored with currants and other nourishing odds and ends.
Saint Elmo's Fire	An optical illusion often reported by sailor and fliers. (There is no such saint.)
Sastrugi	Enormous snowdrifts.
Sennegrass	Tufted marsh grass used as insulation inside of boots and mittens.
Williwaw	A sudden savage squall that comes from the land in the Straits of Magellan and off Cape Horn. The origin of the word is unknown: it may be onomatopoeic.